Sue Fox

Rhodesian Ridgebacks

Everything About Purchase, Care, Nutrition, Behavior, and Training

Filled with Full-color Photographs
Illustrations by Michele Earle-Bridges

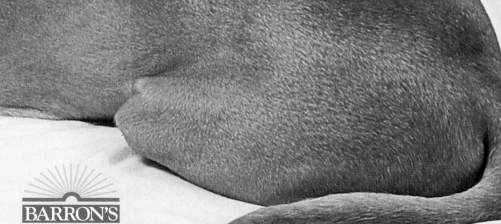

BARRON'S

2 CONTENTS

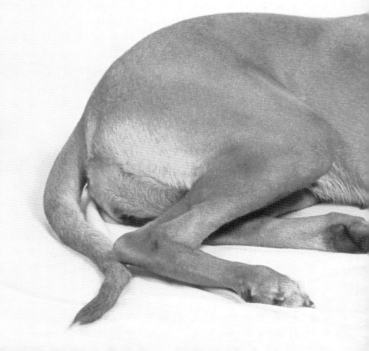

RHODESIAN RIDGEBACK HISTORY

Before the invention of agriculture and permanent settlements, hunter-gatherers domesticated dogs. Although scientists agree that dogs were probably the first domesticated animal, they do not agree on how dogs were domesticated.

Humans and Dogs

One theory postulates that wolves, from which dogs descended, hung around campsites for scraps. Those that learned to be less afraid of people survived and flourished. Those animals developed different traits from wolves, such as tameness, which might have eventually led to trainability. Thus, dogs domesticated themselves through natural selection. Recent research has found that dogs have the ability to pick up on human cues, which probably helps them to function better in human society.

No one knows when dogs originated. However, dogs have an amazing plasticity. They

European settlers in southern Africa developed the Rhodesian Ridgeback in response to their need for a farm dog that could survive in the extreme climate and was also capable of hunting and guarding.

come in a greater variety of shapes, sizes, coat colors, and coat lengths than any other single species of animal. Although they all belong to the same species, *Canis familiaris*, dogs look so different from one another that one might think they were different species.

For thousands of years, people have used selective breeding to retain specific, desirable traits in dogs. So dog breeds developed that varied from one another in size, shape, color, temperament, and behavioral characteristics. Because genetics affects temperament, behavior, and working ability, many breeds almost automatically do the work for which they were bred and appear to enjoy it.

The history of the Rhodesian Ridgeback is linked to European exploration and settlement in Africa. This magnificent breed was developed in response to the unique conditions of its time. These circumstances included guarding the family and livestock and serving as a fearless hunter of lions and other large animals previously unknown to the European settlers.

Development of the Breed

The native ridged dog: The Ridgeback's birthplace began in southern Africa about 450 years ago. The Hottentot or Khoikhoi people occupied the Cape Peninsula of southern Africa when the Dutch established a refueling station for their trading ships on the Cape of Good Hope in 1652. Besides their cattle and sheep, the local people also had a dog that was used for hunting and protection. Historic accounts of this dog are laudatory, recording that the dog was a faithful, fearless, and cunning hunter. The dog was noted for being ferocious when guarding and protecting his owner and possessions. The dog's physique was less highly rated, being called ugly by some. The Hottentot dog was typically less than 18 inches (46 cm) high at the shoulder and described as a lean, hungry-looking mongrel. Early accounts describe a dog with erect ears. Later records, though, describe hanging ears, most likely due to subsequent breeding with dogs of European origin that possessed this trait. The most distinct feature of the Hottentot dog was the line of hair growing in the reverse direction along its back. Within 53 years of the first Dutch settlement, Europeans valued and sought the tough Hottentot dogs for their own use.

When Europeans first immigrated to Africa, they brought livestock and dogs from their native countries. Although the exact types of dogs are unknown, they probably included various kinds of European hunting dogs, bloodhound or scent hound varieties, and Mastiff types for guard purposes. Africa was a harsh country for

the new settlers. Although their dogs did possess outstanding qualities, they were not as tough as the Hottentot dog, which was naturally adapted to the African environment.

The Europeans purposely bred their dogs with the local Hottentot dogs. Numerous unintentional breedings probably also occurred. As a result, the settlers modified their dogs to perform better as hunting and guard dogs under the unique conditions of Africa. Dogs were expected to protect their people from dangerous predators and unfriendly native people. The dogs carrying ridges on their backs became well-known as excellent companions, guard dogs, and hunters. As more settlers arrived, additional breeds of dogs were found in the Cape Province of southern Africa. By the 1860s, Bloodhounds, staghounds, Greyhounds, Bulldogs, terriers, Mastiffs, Pointers, Foxhounds, and crosses among these breeds lived at military outposts and were scattered throughout the frontier. These dog breeds also contributed to the Boer (Dutch) hunting dogs, which were the forerunner of the Rhodesian Ridgeback.

The ridge: The Hottentot was the most important ancestor in the development of the Rhodesian Ridgeback. Its distinguishing feature, the ridge of backward growing hair, likewise marked many, but not all, of the offspring resulting from crosses with the European dogs. Not all early accounts of the Hottentot mention the backward ridge of hair, leaving some breed historians to ponder whether the ridge was not present on all dogs or was so common it was not worth mentioning. Another dog breed with a ridge on its back occurs on the Vietnamese island of Phu Quoc in the Gulf of Thailand. Referred to as the Phu Quoc, it is similar to historic descriptions of the Hottentot. The Thai

Ridgeback is found on the mainland of Thailand and is thought to be a cross between the Phu Quoc and other breeds. Historians tracing the ancestry of the Rhodesian Ridgeback have speculated whether the ridged dogs from Africa were exported to the east, or vice versa, or whether the ridged trait arose independently in two different locations. At this time, no evidence supports one theory over another.

The Ridgebacks were not expected to attack the lion, but would hold it at bay, harassing it until the hunter arrived to make the kill.

The hunting dog: One of the most important recorded steps in the development of the Ridgeback occurred in the 1870s when the Reverend Charles Helm brought two ridged dogs from the Cape Providence in South Africa to the Hope Fountain Mission in Rhodesia (now Zimbabwe). The mission was a place where hunters and travelers stopped for rest and camaraderie. Cornelis van Rooyen, a well-known big-game hunter, saw Reverend Helm's two bitches and admired their looks and guarding abilities. He bred his hunting dogs with them. The result was ridged dogs with red coats and bobbed tails. The offspring formed

top: The unusual ridge of hair growing in the reverse direction to the rest of the coat along the dog's back is the characteristic feature of the Ridgeback.

below: The Rhodesian Ridgeback thrives in wide open spaces.

Ridgebacks were nicknamed "lion dogs" because they helped big game hunters pursue the "king of beasts."

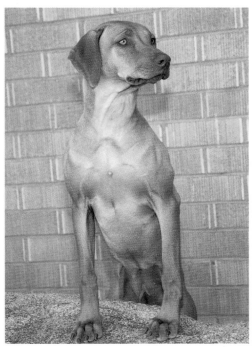

top left: Strong and muscular, the Ridgeback is a powerful, athletic dog that requires daily exercise.

top right: A liver-colored nose is acceptable in the Rhodesian Ridgeback standard.

right: The breeding efforts of the early settlers to South Africa were rewarded with the development of the Rhodesian Ridgeback. The breed combined the best qualities of European dogs and native types to thrive in the rugged environment.

the foundation of van Rooyen's pack of hunting dogs. Over the next 35 years, van Rooyen selectively bred his hunting dogs to produce a dog with the natural ability to bay lions. His dogs became famous and a "lion dog" bred by him was highly coveted. Dogs that were foolhardy were killed by lions and other game animals, thus self-selecting for intelligence. Dogs that were natural guardians were favored with more care and attention by their owners. Hence, the dogs that performed best left more offspring in the next generation.

The hound: The Rhodesian Ridgeback hunting style contains elements of both sight and scent hound types. However, it is classified as a sight hound by the AKC.

Sight hounds work in open landscapes where they chase their prey in full sight. Their long legs, slender bodies, keen sight, great speed, endurance, and desire to kill enable them to catch and kill their quarry without the hunter's help or presence. A slight motion in the distance is often all it takes to arouse their desire to chase.

Scent hounds track their prey by scent, hunting over almost any terrain, and even at night. Surefooted, strong, and fearless, they trail their quarry with loud, continuous vocalizations, allowing the hunter to follow the hunt's progress. Changes in the dogs' vocalizations tell the hunter if the trail is lost, the quarry is being chased, or if it is cornered.

When scent hounds find a good track, they begin to call loudly. They squall continuously while working the track and become quiet only if they lose their quarry's track, whereupon they circle until the track is relocated. When the hounds are chasing the actual quarry, their voices change noticeably in pitch and repetitiveness. When their quarry is run into a den, chased up a tree, or held to the ground, the hounds' voices turn to musical baying. Their continuous baying enables the hunter to locate them, and he or she then assists the hounds by killing the prey.

When hounds are running, a hunter has little influence over them. The hounds have to rely on themselves when confronting an animal or when forcing game to stand or tree, as it can often take hours for the hunter to arrive. Hound dogs in a pack learn how to work as a team from each other. Most hunters start their young hounds with experienced, reliable, older hounds.

The hunting Ridgeback: In the nineteenth century, hunting was more than a means of obtaining food, it became a new pastime. Big-game hunting was an important component of life in Africa, and big-game hunters were celebrated. Hunters needed a dog with the courage and vigor to assist them. The Ridgeback proved to be an outstanding hunter with good scenting ability as well as being an excellent guard dog.

When hunting lions, Ridgebacks were used singly or in a pack. The Ridgeback worked silently on a trail and gave voice only when the lion was run to its den or held to the ground. The Ridgeback did not attack or kill the lion. The dog held the lion at bay by harassing it and darting in and out while staying out of the lion's reach. When the hunter finally arrived, he shot the lion at close range. For such aggressive quarry, the Ridgeback needed agility, tenacity, and aggressiveness.

Ridgebacks did not hunt just lions, they also hunted other species of game animal. Packs of Ridgebacks were used to clear farms of wild pigs and baboons. The Ridgeback could independently kill some quarry, such as baboons, without the assistance of a hunter.

The Breed Is Established

Francis Barnes is credited with spearheading the creation of a breed standard for the ridged dogs. In 1922, he and several other people founded the Rhodesian Ridgeback (Lion Dog) Club of Africa. The club drew up a breed standard to encourage the showing of Ridgebacks and to preserve the characteristics of the breed. The standard was for a handsome dog that retained its primary and natural qualities as a hunting dog. The South African Kennel Union officially recognized the Rhodesian Ridgeback as a breed in 1924.

Prior to creation of the breed standard, the size, color, and coat type of Ridgebacks varied considerably. This was not unexpected considering the large geographic region in which they were found and the variety of dogs that composed the breed. At that time, the people who had ridged dogs were less concerned with how the dogs looked and more concerned with their working ability. Pictures of early Ridgebacks showed variation, such as half-dropped ears.

Ridgebacks were first imported into the United States in the late 1940s. As was typical with many new breeds introduced to the United States after the Second World War, servicepeople brought back dogs found in the countries in which they were stationed. Fanciers of the Rhodesian Ridgeback formed a club and kept records for several generations. In 1955, the American Kennel Club (AKC) recognized the Ridgeback as a purebreed. Ridgebacks have

slowly increased in popularity, but they are still not a well-known breed.

The Rhodesian Ridgeback Standard

A breed standard portrays the ideal specimen; no dog will meet the standard in all respects. In a dog show, the winner is the individual that most closely meets the standard in the judge's opinion. The breed standard is written and governed by the breed's parent club, which is a national organization formed to supervise the breed's welfare.

General Appearance

The Ridgeback represents a strong, muscular, and active dog, symmetrical and balanced in outline. A mature Ridgeback is a handsome, upstanding, and athletic dog, capable of great endurance with a fair amount of speed. Of even, dignified temperament, the Ridgeback is devoted and affectionate to his master, reserved with strangers. The peculiarity of this breed is the ridge on the back. The ridge must be regarded as the characteristic feature of the breed.

Size, Proportion, Substance

A mature Ridgeback should be symmetrical in outline, slightly longer than tall, but well balanced. Dogs—25 to 27 inches (63.5 to 68.6 cm) in height; bitches—24 to 26 inches (61 to 66 cm) in height. Desirable weight: dogs—85 pounds (38.6 kg); bitches—70 pounds (31.8 kg).

The head should be fair in length, with the skull flat and rather broad between the ears. He should be free from wrinkles when in repose. The stop should be reasonably defined.

A Rhodesian Ridgeback is loyal to, affectionate toward, and protective of its human family.

top left: After receiving their daily exercise, Ridgebacks are usually content to relax in the sun.

top right: Rhodesian Ridgebacks are intelligent, but can also be very stubborn.

left: Rhodesian Ridgeback owners know their dogs have a sense of humor.

right: Your Ridgeback puppy will enjoy accompanying you to the beach and mountains.

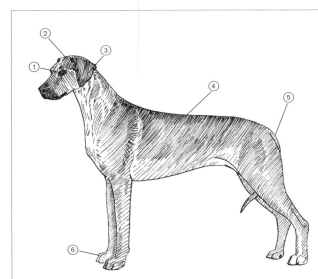

Illustrated Standard

① Round eyes
② Flat skull, rather broad between ears
③ High-set ears of medium size
④ Ridge on back
⑤ Tapering tail, carried with a slight curve
⑥ Feet compact

❏ **Color:** light wheaten to red wheaten; nose can be black, brown, or liver
❏ **DQ:** ridgelessness

The eyes should be moderately well apart. They should be round, bright, and sparkling, with intelligent expression. Their color should harmonize with the color of the dog.

The ears should be set rather high, of medium size, rather wide at the base, and tapering to a rounded point. They should be carried close to the head.

The muzzle should be long, deep, and powerful. The lips should be clean, closely fitting the jaws.

The nose should be black, brown, or liver color, in keeping with the color of the dog. No other colored nose is permissible. A black nose should be accompanied by dark eyes, a brown or liver nose with amber eyes.

The bite: Jaws should be level and strong with well-developed teeth, especially the canines or holders. Scissors bite is preferred.

Neck, Topline, and Body

The neck should be fairly strong and free from throatiness. The chest should not be too wide, but very deep and capacious, ribs moderately well sprung, never rounded like barrel hoops (which would indicate want of speed). The back must be powerful and firm with strong loins, which are muscular and slightly arched. The tail should be strong at the insertion and generally taper toward the end, free from coarseness. It should not be inserted too high or too low and should be carried with a slight curve upward, never curled or gay.

Forequarters

The shoulders should be sloping, clean, and muscular, denoting speed. Elbows should be close to the body. The forelegs should be perfectly straight, strong, and heavy in bone.

The feet should be compact with well-arched toes and round, tough, elastic pads, protected by hair between the toes and pads. Dewclaws may be removed.

Hindquarters

In the hind legs, the muscles should be clean and well-defined, with hocks well down. The feet should be as in front.

Coat

This should be short and dense, sleek and glossy in appearance but neither woolly nor silky.

Color

Light wheaten to red wheaten are acceptable colors. A little white on the chest and toes is permissible, but excessive white there, on the belly, or above the toes is undesirable.

Ridge

The hallmark of this breed is the ridge on the back, which is formed by the hair growing in the opposite direction to the rest of the coat. It should be clearly defined, tapering, and symmetrical. It should start immediately behind the shoulders and continue to a point between the prominence of the hips. It should contain two identical crowns (whorls) directly opposite each other. The lower edge of the crowns should not extend further down the ridge than one-third of the ridge.

Disqualification: Ridgelessness.

Serious fault: One crown or more than two crowns.

Gait

At the trot, the back is held level and the stride is efficient, long, free, and unrestricted. The reach and drive express a perfect balance between power and elegance. At the chase, the Ridgeback demonstrates great coursing ability and endurance.

Temperament

These dogs are dignified and even tempered but reserved with strangers.

UNDERSTANDING YOUR RHODESIAN RIDGEBACK

A dog's role in society has changed in the last fifty years. The relationship between people and dogs has shifted from a working partnership to companionship. Most dogs are now pets. Because fewer dogs are "working dogs," most people now choose a dog for the way it looks rather than for its innate behavioral abilities.

Owning a Rhodesian Ridgeback

There is more to a breed than its looks. Breeds that are chosen to impress other people or because they are trendy often become unwanted because people are unprepared for their other qualities, such as behavior, temperament, and athletic stamina.

Perhaps you are attracted to the Ridgeback because of her handsome looks and fascinating historical legacy as the lion dog. However, this legacy has shaped a dog that is not for everyone. Ridgebacks have a mind of their own, demand a lot of exercise, are physically strong, and need to be part of your family's life.

A Ridgeback can be a demanding breed to own, but living with one can also be personally satisfying.

Trainability

Ridgebacks are sweet and affectionate, but they have a stubborn streak. Their desire to please you is often overridden by their stronger desire to please themselves. Ridgebacks are intelligent, learn quickly, and rarely forget something once it is learned. As long as they are interested in an activity, they will participate. Once it becomes tedious, their willing participation will decline. Unquestioning obedience is not part of their nature.

If a Ridgeback does not want to perform a command, she will not. Then again, when she is doing something she really enjoys, the dog may do it twice. If a Ridgeback does not understand a command, she will often come up with a creative response.

Ridgebacks can be masters of selective hearing. Furthermore, they know that you cannot correct them when they are off leash and you are far away. Such spontaneity is appealing to some people, but others find variable responses and a battle of wills irritating. Ridgebacks are sensitive, and severe training methods can ruin their trust. If you lose your temper, you will have to work long and hard to regain your Ridgeback's trust, and she will never forget. They respond best to kindness, clarity, humor, and respect, not coercion.

Because they can present a training challenge, Ridgebacks are not the best choice for an inexperienced dog owner. If you like the challenge of working with a confident, independent dog, though, you will enjoy the Ridgeback.

Part of the Family

Ridgebacks are loyal, family dogs and thrive on attention and affection from their family. They cannot be left outside, neglected in a backyard with only occasional attention. They must be part of your family. Ridgebacks require daily attention and human companionship. Do not expect your Ridgeback to lie quietly in a corner across the room from you. When you sit on the couch with your feet on the table, your Ridgeback will lie beneath your legs. If your Ridgeback is allowed on the couch, she will lie down so that she is touching you, or she will lie draped over your lap.

Expect your Ridgeback to watch you and shadow you. When you go to another room, your Ridgeback will follow you, even pushing into the bathroom. Ridgebacks are not weekend dogs. If you are gone at work all day and go out most nights, the Ridgeback is not a suitable choice. The Ridgeback is ideal for someone who truly wants a canine companion integrated into his or her life. Within his

family, the Ridgeback will closely bond with one person.

The breed standard states that Ridgebacks are reserved with strangers. Until your dog gets to know someone, she will usually be standoffish. Ridgebacks socialized as youngsters with many new people in friendly settings, such as dog parks or family gatherings, might be more sociable and outgoing toward strangers. However, the breed does not naturally seek attention from unfamiliar people.

Exercise and Activity Level

Ridgebacks need exercise every day. They have impressive stamina and endurance. They are a good breed for people who have an active lifestyle and want a canine companion to accompany them on long walks, hikes, bike rides, cross-country ski tours, and horseback rides. Swimming is another option for some Ridgebacks. Some individuals love to swim, but many will only get their feet wet.

A fenced yard is necessary, but it is no substitute for interactive exercise with you. Few dogs will run and play by themselves in a yard. They usually wait for their owner. Your dog needs not just exercise but also your companionship. Even when multiple dogs are kept together, most of their high-energy play will take place when their owner is present, not when the dogs are by themselves.

Ridgebacks are not good apartment dogs. However, resourceful city dwellers who live near a dog park that allows dogs off leash can successfully care for a Ridgeback. City living requires dedicated owners willing to provide their Ridgeback with numerous daily outings.

An active breed like the Ridgeback is a lot of work because, rain or shine, the dog still needs her daily exercise. Without enough exercise, your Ridgeback might find destructive ways to burn her energy. A bored Ridgeback might dig holes in the backyard or try to escape from the yard in search of more interesting things to do. Even a 6-foot (1.8-m) fence can be scaled by a determined Ridgeback. A walk around one or two blocks on a leash at the end of the day might not suffice. The breed does best when provided with opportunities to run off leash. Once they have had their exercise, though, they are content being couch potatoes and lap dogs.

A younger family member might not have the size and strength to control a strong, powerful Ridgeback. Even adults can lose their hold on the leash if a Ridgeback sees something she wants to chase. Of course, such unruly behavior is less likely in a well-trained Ridgeback, but you still must consider whether you are able to handle a large dog.

Behavior

The Ridgeback has a well-developed protective instinct, which was valued and cultivated by the breed's developers in Africa. The Ridgeback has a deep, resounding bark but is not excessively vocal or given to nuisance barking. She will typically bark only when there is a disturbance, warranting your investigation, such as people at the door, delivery trucks, other dogs, or people walking by your home. An adult will consider your home and yard her

Children and Ridgebacks can become the best of friends.

territory and act protective around it. Although they are good watchdogs, they are not guard dogs and are unlikely to attack a person.

Your Ridgeback takes cues from you. If you are not concerned when a visitor comes over, neither will your dog be. Stories of the intuitive protective abilities and actions of the Ridgeback abound. Some are fanciful, others a testament to the dog's natural abilities. One of the more frequently reported behaviors occurs when an unfamiliar visitor stands up or makes a quick move, resulting in the Ridgeback moving between her owner and the visitor.

Protective behavior should not be exhibited in puppies. It will naturally appear near the onset of sexual maturity. You may never encounter circumstances where your Ridgeback's protective behavior is exhibited, since it should surface only under appropriate circumstances. Some dogs are more protective and emit a low, menacing growl when a stranger approaches the home or their owners but

top left: A fenced yard is necessary. The fence must be at least six feet high to prevent your Ridgeback from jumping over it.

top right: Your Rhodesian Ridgeback will consider your backyard as his territory.

left: Ridgebacks and children can get along well together, but both must be taught how to behave around one another.

The Ridgeback
is an alert,
confident dog.

Ridgebacks enjoy
socializing with
other friendly
dogs.

Many Ridgebacks are watchful of "their" children.

should stop when told. You do not want your dog to act aggressively toward someone you have invited into your home; neither do you want your children's friends to be your dog's enemies. Some people worry that if they limit their dog's protective behavior she will cease to be protective or will not be protective when necessary. However, this is an innate behavior with Ridgebacks and does not need to be cultivated.

Ridgebacks are good with children and enjoy their company. However, like any dog, a Ridgeback who has never met a child is less likely to exhibit such tendencies. Because Ridgebacks are a large, strong breed, they must be taught to interact properly with a variety of people, including children (see page 42). Young, energetic Ridgebacks can be exuberant. They might accidentally run into a small child or whack them with their tails. Some Ridgebacks seem to behave more gently around children intuitively, but others must be taught how to

behave. Children must also be taught to be respectful and kind to the dog. Dogs of any breed should never be left unsupervised with infants or toddlers.

Other pets: If properly introduced while still a puppy, most Ridgebacks readily accept other household pets. However, experiences with other pets, for example, cats and small animals such as rabbits, vary. Because they were bred to hunt, some Ridgebacks might be more inclined to chase or attack another pet. Although introductions work best when your dog is still a puppy, many adult dogs can be trained to accept another animal as a member of the family. Supervise any introduction and the initial interactions. Make sure the animals are fine with one another before you leave them alone together.

Ridgebacks do not tend to be pushy or dominant around other dogs. Depending on how they were socialized, most are friendly with other dogs. Always pay attention when two dogs meet for the first time. Situations can develop where a fight might occur. Intact males are less likely to back down when challenged by other dogs, although this tendency varies by individual.

Other traits: In general, Ridgebacks, like other sight hounds, have little fear or respect for moving cars. If they see a squirrel or cat in the distance, some Ridgebacks will bolt and chase the animal. While pursuing their prey, they can be deaf to the world around them, including your calls and approaching cars. Most Ridgebacks are perfectly reliable off leash. However, use common sense. Train your Ridgeback to wait to exit a car until you give the signal, and never let her charge out the front door. Keep the dog on lead when around roads.

The Ridgeback considers any food left on countertops or tabletops to be hers for the taking. Protect your Ridgeback from her opportunistic nature by placing any food out of her reach. Training a Ridgeback to stay out of the kitchen and dining area is one effective way to prevent her from poaching your food.

Ridgebacks are tough dogs but not so tough that they can stay outside unprotected in cold climates. When in good physical condition, Ridgebacks have little subcutaneous fat. This plus their short coat make them less hardy in cold climates. If your Ridgeback must spend part of the day outside in cold weather, you must provide her with a heated doghouse. Alternatively, a dog door will give your Ridgeback a method to go outside when you are not home. Ridgebacks do love bounding through the snow, but they also appreciate the chance to come back inside and get warm. A dog sweater or coat can increase your dog's comfort in cold weather. A cold Ridgeback will appreciate being covered with a blanket while she snoozes on her bed.

Male or Female

The main differences between the sexes are related to size. Male Ridgebacks are taller and heavier than the female (85 pounds [38.6 kg] compared with 70 pounds [31.8 kg], on average). Additionally, the male should look more powerful than the female and have a larger head. In comparison, the female should be more elegant and feminine while still being

Life Span

The life span of Ridgebacks ranges from about ten to twelve years, although some live up to fifteen years of age. Ridgebacks are a slow maturing breed and do not reach their full size until they are almost two years old. While their maximum height is reached by one year of age, they continue to fill out for another year.

muscular. Both sexes are affectionate and loyal, and any slight differences between them do not affect these traits. No significant training or obedience differences exist between the sexes. Among those who still use Ridgebacks for hunting, it is sometimes thought that the females are better than the males because they are slightly quicker and more aggressive.

Male dogs lift their leg to urinate and mark their territory. Hence, the trees and bushes in your yard will be marked from his belly height down. Females squat on the ground and tend to urinate all at once, rather than marking multiple locations. Compared with neutered males, intact males are more concerned with marking their territory. Walking an intact male around the block can take considerably longer than a female since he will want to stop and mark every few yards. If you have patio furniture or other items in your yard, you may or may not be able to teach your male not to mark them. A male puppy does not begin to lift his leg to urinate until he is almost six months old, and some do not do so until they are a year old.

Both neutered and intact male dogs are more likely than females to mount other dogs for sexual satisfaction and to show dominance.

Young Ridgebacks are boisterous and playful.

Male Ridgebacks (left) are larger than females.

Making time for vigorous off-leash play is essential for a Ridgeback's health and happiness.

If your Ridgeback's sole purpose in life is to be a companion, have it spayed or neutered. You will be glad you did.

The other dog will express its displeasure by growling or snapping, which is usually sufficient to cause the male to dismount. Males might also try to hump a person's leg. This unacceptable behavior can be stopped by removing him and in a firm, no-nonsense tone telling him *"No."*

Any differences between males and females are most apparent in dogs that are not neutered or spayed. Intact males can be more difficult to control and command. If not kept in a fenced area, they are more likely to roam. They can also become dominant and aggressive toward other males and are more likely to fight with other intact male dogs. These traits do not usually appear until the male is at least one year old. Neutering can eliminate these behavioral difficulties, and neutered males generally have a longer life span than intact males.

An unspayed female will come into season or heat for approximately three weeks twice a year. Females in season can be messy and sometimes moody. During this time, a female is receptive to intact males and can become pregnant. Because she is feeling amorous, your female might try to escape your yard to find a male. Free-roaming, unneutered males will congregate at your home to try mating with the female.

More than One Puppy

Do not buy more than one puppy. Training two puppies at the same time is almost impossible. Difficulties arise when you must discipline one puppy without the other wincing because she thinks you are also scolding her. While training one puppy to listen to you, you can be training the other puppy to not listen to you. Two puppies will get into twice as much trouble as one. Knowing which puppy was the mischief maker can be difficult. If a mess is made in the house, you will not know which puppy needs more help with housebreaking.

Other problems can arise with two puppies. Different dogs have different temperaments. One may respond rapidly to training, while the other requires much more work to learn the same behaviors. Two puppies will bond with each other, not with you. Moreover, they will constantly battle for the top-dog position as they get older. One puppy might always lose, which can cause her to become insecure while the winner might have an overinflated sense of her status that other dogs do not recognize.

Finding enough time to spend with one puppy can be hard, let alone spending individual time with two. If you are concerned about your puppy being lonely, arranging play sessions with a

Your adult Ridgeback will want to accompany you wherever you go.

Rhodesian Ridgebacks at a Glance

Listed below are some of the most important traits that you should consider when choosing a purebred dog to share your life. The Rhodesian Ridgeback's ranking for each trait is listed below. Carefully consider whether the Ridgeback is the right breed for you. Consider whether you can meet the dog's requirements and whether your expectations match the breed's needs.

Trait	High	Moderate	Low
Energy Level		X	
Exercise Needs	X		
Friendliness		X	
Playfulness		X	
Affection Level		X	
Watchdog Ability	X		
Trainability		X	
Grooming Needs			X
Good with Children	X		

neighbor's or friend's dog is much easier than caring for a second puppy. Wait until she is grown, well socialized, and obedience trained before getting your puppy a playmate. If you get another puppy to keep your present dog company, you will need to devote just as much time to housebreaking and training her as you did for your first dog. In addition, you will still have to provide sufficient exercise and attention to your first dog.

SELECTING A RHODESIAN RIDGEBACK

What do dogs require? Time, and lots of it. You can consider all kinds of traits when selecting which breed is best for you, but the one factor that changes little is the daily time a dog requires. Some independent breeds might require less of your time, but the Ridgeback requires a lot of time.

Should You Own a Dog?

If you expect your dog to sit quietly at home, be there when you desire, but otherwise be no trouble or imposition, a dog is not for you. Owning a dog is a huge responsibility. A dog depends completely on you. If you do not have enough time, a better choice for a pet might be the more independent cat. Caring for a dog should be fun, not a chore. If you love dogs, the time spent training, socializing, and playing is time well spent. If you think your interest and commitment might wane, reconsider your decision to get a dog.

Dogs can be expensive. Besides the initial purchase price of your Ridgeback, there are toys,

Bringing home a new puppy is exciting, but caring for your puppy is a lot of work.

beds, food, and veterinary expenses. Routine veterinary costs, such as annual checkups and vaccinations, are predictable and easy to calculate. However, the cost for unexpected veterinary care is unpredictable. Whether an emergency or a long-term chronic condition, count on unexpected veterinary bills.

Exercise

The Ridgeback needs exercise and social stimulation. Many behavioral problems in Ridgebacks occur because the dogs are left alone all day and find destructive ways to amuse themselves.

Without you: If you cannot always provide enough exercise, dog walkers and dog day care can make owning a dog easier. Using these services will not make your dog any less devoted to you but can actually make your canine companion healthier and more pleasurable to be around. When you come home from work, your Ridgeback will be calmer and less likely to have gotten into mischief if he has had some exercise earlier in the day.

Dog walkers will walk your dog singly or as part of a group. Be sure to check references. A dog day care facility should be clean and have knowledgeable staff. Do inquire about the facility's level of supervision, what kinds of behavior are tolerated, any scheduled activities, and policies regarding current vaccinations. Be sure to visit the facility and check references before leaving your dog. These services can be expensive, but using them two to three times a week is often sufficient for your Ridgeback.

Other exercise options for your Ridgeback include a trustworthy friend or neighbor who loves dogs but does not have one of his or her own. If a friend or neighbor is interested in including your dog while jogging, walking, or hiking, be sure the person is knowledgeable about dogs and knows how to handle your dog. Paying a responsible older teenager to walk your dog is another possibility. Younger children, however, are physically less capable of handling a large, powerful Ridgeback.

If you live near a dog park, your Ridgeback can get regular off-leash exercise as well as the opportunity to play with other dogs. Sitting and visiting with other owners while your Ridgeback expends his energy in a fun, nondestructive manner can be relaxing. Of course, you must pay attention to the dog dynamics to prevent any fights.

Dog friends: Some people whose dogs are "good friends" arrange to drop one dog off at the other's home so the dogs can play together during the day. Make sure their fenced yard is as safely enclosed and dog proofed as your own. Sometimes, though, dogs do not play as enthusiastically unless they have an audience.

When to Get Your Ridgeback

Bringing home a new puppy is exciting, but it also means a commitment of time and energy, especially during the first few weeks. Plan to acquire your puppy when you will have the maximum amount of time available for his care. In some parts of the country, the time of year might affect your decision on when to acquire your puppy. Housebreaking a puppy in cold, snowy weather can be difficult. Both you and your puppy are likely to be miserable if the outside temperatures are freezing.

Expect to make a large commitment of time the first year of your Ridgeback puppy's life. During the first year, you will housebreak him, take him to obedience classes, and socialize him so your dog is used to a variety of people and places. The initial training requires great effort but has tremendous rewards; you are developing the foundation for a companion who will share your life for the next 10 to 15 years. Your investment in time can prevent the development of undesirable, bad habits in your Ridgeback.

Where to Buy Your Ridgeback

The best place to begin your search for a Ridgeback is the web site of the Ridgeback Club of America, which can provide lists of breeders in your area. Ridgebacks are not a common breed, and you might have to travel out of your area to obtain a puppy. No matter where you buy your puppy, trust your instincts and do not rush. You are choosing a companion who will share your home for the next decade.

Be aware of two conditions that can affect Ridgeback puppies: lack of ridges and dermoid sinuses. Some Ridgeback puppies are born without the breed's characteristic ridge. The ridge will not develop as the puppy matures. Breeders historically culled ridgeless puppies, but some now offer them for sale as pets. A dog without a ridge still has the breed's other characteristics and will make a fine pet. But ridgeless dogs cannot compete in conformation shows or lure coursing; they can compete in obedience, agility, and tracking. Dermoid sinus is a potentially fatal condition that is present at birth in some Ridgeback puppies. This condition is discussed on page 85. Be sure the puppy you are considering has been screened by a knowledgeable veterinarian or breeder.

Reputable Breeders

Reputable breeders know the Ridgeback and invest in genetic screening. They will have their dogs' hips and elbows x-rayed and rated by the Orthopedic Foundation for Animals (OFA) or by the University of Pennsylvania (PennHIP). Doing so will reduce the incidence of these hereditary conditions. Hips and elbows cannot be certified by these organizations until the dog is two years old. Thus, the dam and sire should be at least two years of age. Some breeders also have their dogs' eyes examined and cleared by a veterinary ophthalmologist affiliated with the Canine Eye Registration Foundation (CERF). Knowledgeable breeders screen for other potential hereditary diseases, such as dermoid sinuses. While problems can occur in a serious breeder's stock, they are much less likely. Such breeders are interested in and will keep track of

any hereditary problems that result from specific pairings.

Breeders of high-quality puppies will have spent time and money proving that the sire and dam are physically and mentally sound. The dogs they breed are likely to have show points or championship titles. To produce the best possible puppies, they will match pedigrees and abilities. They will raise their puppies in a warm, clean environment and socialize them so they do not have preventable temperament problems.

Serious breeders who show their dogs and compete in obedience competitions usually have waiting lists for puppies. Individuals on the waiting list eagerly await certain breedings. In many cases, all the puppies from a given breeding are already sold before they are even whelped.

Reputable breeders will usually ask you questions to make sure a Ridgeback will fit your lifestyle. The breeder will want to know about you and how prepared you are for the puppy. Breeders feel responsible for the puppies they breed and want to make sure they are placed in the best home possible. If you cannot keep your dog at any time during his life, the breeder will often take back the dog and find him a new home. A good breeder will also be available to answer any questions you might have about your puppy.

Backyard Breeders

Backyard breeder is a derogatory term that refers to someone who casually breeds dogs without researching the dogs' backgrounds. These are individuals who own a pet dog and breed it with someone else's pet dog without regard to health or temperament. Although some are well-intentioned, other individuals can be unscrupulous and interested in money

A reputable breeder can help you choose which puppy will best fit with your family and lifestyle.

more than in the welfare of the puppies or breed. Backyard breeders are less likely to have screened the dam and sire for hereditary problems, and they might not even know that they should screen their dogs. They also might not be aware of potential problems in their puppies, such as dermoid sinuses, which can cause you much heartbreak and expense.

Puppies from backyard breeders are typically less expensive than those from a reputable breeder. If you choose to buy your Ridgeback from a casual breeder, make sure the sire and dam have been certified by the Orthopedic Foundation for Animals for hips and elbows

rated at least "good" and that the puppies were checked by a knowledgeable veterinarian for dermoid sinuses.

Puppies that are advertised in the classified section of newspapers are typically from backyard breeders. Do not put too much importance on the statement "champion bloodlines." It does not mean the parents are champions. It usually means a couple of champions might be in the puppies' pedigree, but they are often several generations back. One can often obtain a reasonable pet-quality dog from a backyard breeder, but you are not likely to find a show-quality puppy.

Getting a healthy puppy should be your first concern.

Other Important Details

Show or Pet Quality

Experienced breeders will usually rate the puppies in a litter as either show or pet quality. Breeders can make only an educated guess about a puppy's show potential, based on their years of experience. When compared with the littermates who are rated pet quality, a show-quality puppy possesses certain features such as soundness of construction, balance (how the puppy is put together), and a ridge that conforms to the breed's standard. Such puppies might also stand out with a confident disposition. However, the breeder cannot guarantee a puppy's show potential.

Nothing is wrong with a pet-quality puppy. He just possesses features that would make it difficult to compete successfully in conformation shows, such as an imperfect ridge. However, these showring faults do not affect the puppy's ability to function. Likewise, a kinked tail or too much white on the chest or feet will not affect the puppy's ability to live a long, happy life as a pet.

Important Papers

When you buy your puppy, the breeder will give you a copy of the puppy's pedigree, a registration application, and sometimes a sales contract. Some breeders may also provide you with copies of the hip and elbow clearance for your puppy's parents.

A pedigree is a chronological list of your puppy's ancestors for three or more generations. It will show the registered names of your puppy's ancestors. The CH before a dog's name

Your Ridgeback must be part of your life; this breed should not be left alone in the yard for long periods of time.

means the dog is a show champion. The more often you see CH on both the maternal and paternal sides of your puppy's ancestry, the more likely your puppy is to meet the breed standard. Titles in recent generations are more meaningful than those several generations back.

To register your puppy as yours, you must fill in and mail the registration application to the AKC. In order to show your Ridgeback, he must be registered with the AKC. Some breeders offer AKC Limited Registration, which is a tool to protect the breed. Dogs with Limited Registration are ineligible for competition in dog shows and breeding (i.e., any offspring could not be subsequently registered with the AKC). However, the dogs can still compete in obedience and other performance activities. Because puppies without registration papers cannot be sold for as much money, this provides less motivation for pet owners to breed purely for profit.

Some breeders provide a written sales contract that states what health and temperament guarantees they offer. Some sales contracts contain a spaying or neutering clause, which requires you to have your puppy fixed when he or she is old enough. Reputable breeders are protective of their kennel name; they do not want pet-quality dogs from their kennel being bred.

Price

A Ridgeback is relatively expensive. Expect to spend between $400 to $600 dollars. Show-quality puppies or those from champion parents will cost even more. Expect to pay for a breeder's investment in the breed. You might think you cannot afford to buy from a good breeder, but the expense of veterinary bills from a poorly bred dog can make the initial purchase price seem insignificant.

How Old?

The best age to acquire your Ridgeback puppy is eight weeks of age. By seven weeks of age, puppies begin to take an active interest in playing and interacting with people. By eight weeks, the puppy is ready to learn and needs human company and stimulation.

What to Look For

The breeder's home or kennel should be clean with no offensive odors. You should always be able to see the mother, called the *dam,* but you might not be able to see the father, called the *sire,* because he may live out of the area. However, the breeder can show you photographs of the sire and tell you about him, such as his height, weight, and whether he has any titles or points toward a championship.

The puppies should be clean and free of odor. A healthy puppy will feel robust and solid and have a clean, glossy coat. He should not feel frail and bony or have a bloated belly. Long toenails and a dull coat indicate a lack of care. Make sure the puppies have clean eyes and noses and that their ears have no discharge or unpleasant odor. The puppies should be well socialized and confident. Make sure the sales terms include your veterinarian's confirmation of the puppy's good health.

Avoid choosing a puppy from the two behavioral extremes: the shy puppy who hides or is overly submissive and the bold puppy who shoves his way ahead of the others to visit with you. Do not feel sorry for the underdog. Puppies that are submissive can grow up to be tentative, fearful adults. They need an experienced owner who knows how to cultivate their confidence. The boldest puppy is attractive, but such an

Take your time when deciding which puppy to bring home.

individual is likely to be the dominant one in the litter and the toughest to train. A bold puppy will also require more effort and time to keep occupied. Dominant puppies grow up to be adults with dominant personalities. Without an experienced owner, they can be pushy and difficult to control.

Allow the breeder to help you select your puppy. Experienced, conscientious breeders are interested in making the best possible match for each puppy and new owner, and they are skilled at doing so. They know each puppy's character and personality and will know which puppy is best suited to your family.

Consider an Adult Dog

Older puppies and adult dogs are available for adoption through local and national Ridgeback rescue groups (see page 92). A Ridgeback might need a new home because of divorce, death, a family move, or lack of time. Rescue groups typically screen dogs for health problems and temperament before placing them for adoption and work to make the best fit between an adopter and dog.

If you want to bypass some of the difficult puppy stages such as housebreaking, teething, and chewing, consider an older dog. Older dogs have numerous advantages over puppies, including being less interested in exploring

everything with their mouths. Once they settle into your home and way of life, rescue dogs often make loyal pets. However, you must be patient because they are not always free of problems. Adult dogs can be more set in their ways, and some might have bothersome habits such as begging or barking. A disobedient puppy can also be easier to contend with than a disobedient adult Ridgeback.

You can also contact reputable breeders to see whether they know of any available retired show dogs or older puppies who did not fulfill their early potential as show prospects. Consider an older puppy only if he was raised in a home environment, not outside in a kennel. Finally, if you do not have the ability to make a full-time commitment to a dog, consider contacting a rescue group to provide temporary foster care for a rescued Ridgeback.

Before you bring home your puppy, you should purchase a crate, bed, collar, leash, identification tag, food and water bowls, and toys.

What Your Puppy Needs

Your Rhodesian Ridgeback puppy is a baby, and like any other baby, its needs must be fully addressed if it is to grow into a well-adjusted adult. While caring for the puppy, remember the adult this dog will become and establish its place in the family "pack" at the very beginning.

Crate

A crate is essential. Some pet owners, especially first-time owners, are reluctant to use a crate because they think it is a cruel cage. However, not only will a crate help you keep your sanity, but your puppy will see the crate as her own private bedroom or den and a safe place in which to retreat. Crate training is also advantageous if your dog ever needs to travel by air since she will already be used to a crate.

When you first bring your puppy home, he might be frightened or overwhelmed by his new surroundings.

A crate is invaluable in housebreaking, discussed in detail on page 46. Although dogs are den animals and generally do not eliminate in their dens or sleeping areas, puppies may soil at the end of the crate farthest from their sleeping area if the crate is too large. If you buy an adult-sized crate, you might need to reduce the crate's size temporarily by blocking off a portion with a piece of plywood or a large, snug-fitting cardboard box.

If necessary, encourage your puppy to use her crate by placing toys or food treats at the back of the crate. Place an inexpensive blanket inside. When some puppies teethe, they might chew the bedding. Ripped and shredded bedding will still provide a comfortable nest for the puppy. However, she could accidentally swallow a piece of bedding, which might cause a digestive blockage. Providing her with an alternative chew toy inside her crate, such as a hard bone, can help prevent this potential problem.

Do not misuse the crate. The crate is a safe refuge, not a prison or a place of punishment. Do not leave your puppy unattended in her crate for more than a few hours. Older puppies between three to four months of age should not be left for more than three to four hours. Do not lock your puppy in her crate when she is boisterous and needs to run and play. If you are away from home all day, you will not be able to leave your puppy in her crate unless someone is available to take the puppy outside *regularly* every few hours and also to play with her. If you need a few moments of free time, you can put your puppy in her crate as long as you provide her with a suitable chew toy or other item to play with.

You must decide right away whether you will use a crate for your puppy. An older, adolescent puppy is less likely to accept a crate as her den and will have a fit if you suddenly try to confine her in a crate.

The Puppy Room

If you do not use a crate, you must confine your puppy to a safe room within your home. Typically, the kitchen or bathroom is best because they have tile or linoleum floors that are easy to keep clean. Because you want the puppy to be part of your family, the kitchen is usually best. Be sure the cupboards are securely closed. Move any poisonous products safely out of reach in case your puppy does open a cupboard. Use a puppy or child's gate to keep her in the room.

This method does have disadvantages. Your puppy can wake up before you do and eliminate. Therefore, you may need to paper-train your puppy. While paper-training can delay the housebreaking process, it can help to keep things tidier in the interim. Confine your puppy to a small room or partition an area of the room. Make sure the space is large enough so your puppy will not have to eliminate near her bed, food, or water bowls. Cover the floor with newspaper. You can eventually reduce the area covered because the puppy will always use one spot. This method has disadvantages because it does allow a puppy to eliminate in the house. Furthermore, puppies show great discrimination when it comes to surfaces and might prefer to use newspapers rather than dirt or grass. If this problem develops, place some newspaper on the ground outside.

Bed

Provide your puppy with a comfortable bed or a nest of blankets in which she can rest, sleep, and chew her toys. The bed can be in addition to her crate, or can fit inside her crate. Either way, choose a bed with a removable cover so that it, like the blankets, can be easily washed.

You will need to buy new collars and leashes as your puppy outgrows the old ones.

A tattoo is a permanent means of identifying your dog.

Collar

Purchase a flat-buckle collar for your puppy. Your puppy might initially scratch at her collar, but she will soon get used to it. A puppy will outgrow several collars before she has finished growing. Some economical collars are designed to expand as your puppy grows and can last for many months before a new one is needed. For proper fit, two fingers should readily fit between the collar and your puppy's neck. A collar is necessary to attach your puppy's identification and leash. Do not use a choke collar for these purposes; it is a training tool.

Identification

Immediately attach some type of identification tag with your address and telephone number to your puppy's collar. Identification tags can accidentally fall off. It is prudent to write your phone number in permanent marker directly on your puppy's collar.

More sophisticated methods of identification include inserting a microchip the size of a grain of rice under the dog's skin at the base of the neck and tattooing. Many veterinary hospitals and shelter facilities have scanners for the microchips, which can identify the dog and the owner's relevant information. A tattoo is usually done on the inside of a dog's thigh. You can have your dog tattooed with your social security number or AKC number. If you use your social security number, for a small fee you can register your dog with the National Registry. Because these methods are not readily interpreted by a stranger who finds your dog,

an identification tag affixed to your dog's collar is still recommended.

Leash

Most basic obedience classes require a 6-foot (1.8-m) leash, not a 4-foot (1.2-m) leash. A nylon, cotton-webbed, or leather leash are all good choices. Do not purchase a leash with a large metal clip that is too heavy or uncomfortable for your puppy. You can always buy the leash of your dreams when your puppy is larger.

Pooper-scooper

If your puppy will be confined to a backyard for her bathroom area, a pooper-scooper is indispensable. This long-handled tool can make cleaning up much easier and quicker compared with a shovel. No dog likes to play or lounge in a dirty yard. Besides being smelly, droppings are prime breeding grounds for flies. Viruses and intestinal parasites are also transmitted through droppings. Furthermore, a young, frolicking puppy might accidentally step in her droppings and then track them into the house.

When taking your dog for a walk, a plastic bag is the easiest device to clean up after your dog. Place the bag over the dropping, pick up the dropping, and then turn the bag inside out. Your hand will always be protected by the plastic bag. Not only is cleanup required in some areas, doing so will win you the appreciation of your neighbors.

Toys

Your puppy needs her own toys, and shopping for puppy toys is fun. Just because a toy is made for dogs does not mean it is safe. By nature, puppies teethe and destroy items, so carefully choose your puppy's toys. Puppies often enjoy carrying around, sleeping with, and thrashing a soft stuffed toy. However, many older puppies are gifted at disemboweling their stuffed toys, potentially swallowing some of the stuffing and even the squeaker. Supervise your puppy's play with any toy that she can destroy and eat. Sterilized natural bones, nylon bones, and toys made of hard, indestructible rubber are fine for your

Puppies love soft fleece toys.

puppy to chew when she is alone. Rawhide chews of various shapes and sizes are safe for many Ridgeback puppies. However, limit the number you offer if your puppy quickly devours the rawhides (see page 63).

Too many toys might confuse your puppy. Most puppies enjoy a few hard toys and one soft stuffed toy. As your puppy grows, you can slowly expand her toy collection. Play with your puppy and her toys, but do not play tug-of-war. Doing so encourages your puppy to bite harder and is also thought to encourage dominance behavior. Do not encourage your puppy to use her mouth on your hand or clothes; give her a toy instead. Practice saying *"Give"* so that your puppy learns to release her toy to you or other family members.

The First Days at Home

The first few days at home with your new puppy will be happy, exciting, and memorable. However, there are several important things that you must do for her health and well-being.

To the Veterinarian

During her first scheduled visit, your veterinarian should be able to detect any serious structural problems that could adversely affect your puppy. Ideally, within the first 24 hours, your puppy should be examined by your veterinarian. The veterinarian will check for conditions such as heart murmurs, infections, bite and teeth alignment, and hernias and will review a vaccination schedule. If possible, bring a fresh stool sample so your puppy can be checked for internal parasites.

Watch your puppy to make sure he does not get into mischief.

The First Few Nights

You might not sleep too soundly the first few nights your puppy is home. Expect to let her sleep inside her crate or a large cardboard sleeping box with the top opened in your bedroom for the first week. Later on, you can move her crate or sleeping box into the hall and then into another room (although Ridgebacks are happiest sharing their owners' bedroom). Keeping her next to your bed at night can help your puppy adjust to her new life. You will hear her if she wakes up whimpering and frightened and can quietly reassure her. Persistent crying is likely to be an emergency signal indicating she needs to be taken outside to eliminate. The puppy must adjust to your life, but allowances must be made for her needs. You do not want to encourage 2:00 A.M. play sessions, so after she has voided, return her to her crate. She will soon fall asleep. Feeding your puppy her last meal earlier in the evening might reduce the need for any midnight outings, although your puppy might also just wake up earlier in the morning.

Safety Considerations

You must puppy proof your home. Potentially hazardous items, such as poisonous houseplants, household cleaning products, and medicines, must be moved out of reach. Electrical cords must be taped safely out of the way. Puppies explore the world with their

Puppies investigate everything with their mouths.

mouths and need to chew. Anything left lying on the floor will be tested by your puppy's mouth. These items must be picked up and put out of reach until your puppy knows not to chew them. To a puppy, children's toys can look just like her own. However, seldom are such

A wide variety of toys is available for your puppy.

toys sturdy enough for a puppy. If the puppy swallows toy pieces, they can cause digestive problems and an expensive veterinary bill. Until she knows better, keep an unsupervised puppy out of the children's room and help your youngsters pick up their toys.

You should confine your puppy to one or two rooms where you can watch her. Close the doors to the other rooms, and block off access to the rest of the house with inside gates.

Life with a Puppy

A Ridgeback puppy is active and playful. Your puppy will bounce around, wild and rambunctious, and then will suddenly be fast asleep napping. Your puppy needs to learn your rules with a minimum of stress and emotional trauma. Have patience. Help her channel her energy into acceptable activities so she does not destroy things. Do not encourage behavior in your puppy that would be unacceptable for an adult dog. Now is the time for your puppy to get used to being touched all over, including her mouth, ears, and feet.

Between 7 to 12 weeks, your puppy will be cuddly and dependent on you. During this time, your puppy has a high learning potential. Between 12 and 16 weeks, she will assert her own will and desires, becoming more mischievous and potentially destructive. At this age, you can train her for longer periods. Adolescence begins around four to five months when the puppy loses his baby teeth. This period can last until the puppy is between seven to nine months of age. Like a moody teenager, your puppy will have days of rebelliousness, insecurity, and so forth. You might need to reinforce basic obedience commands rather than working on new ones. Be patient—your puppy will eventually grow up.

When you take your puppy outside to play in your fenced backyard, watch her for the first few times. A puppy might eat flowers, shrubs, and lawn furniture and find other hazards and ways to escape that you might not know about. Some backyard plants are poisonous. Lists of poisonous plants are available from many references and should be reviewed to make sure toxic plants are not in your yard.

Young puppies have trouble walking up and down stairs. You will need to carry your puppy until she is big enough to negotiate any stairs on her own safely. Do not overexercise your new puppy even as she grows in size and becomes more exuberant. Check with your veterinarian for the appropriate age to increase his exercise regimen.

Children and the Puppy

Both children and a puppy must learn how to behave around one another. Ridgeback puppies have sharp teeth that can frighten children if they play-bite. Puppies tend to jump and their sharp nails can scratch unprotected skin. As a Ridgeback puppy grows bigger, she can accidentally knock over or hurt a small child.

An adult should supervise the puppy and children to be sure they interact safely and appropriately. Children must learn not to encourage the puppy to run after them, and the puppy must learn not to chase and jump on children. Do not allow children to be rough or allow the puppy to nip. If your puppy is teething, have the children give her a toy on which to gnaw, not their hands or clothes. Children sometimes tease a puppy by wiggling their fingers in front of the puppy's face or by taking away a toy and then repeatedly tempting her with it. Children must be taught to not tease the puppy. When a dog does not want to be bothered, she will get up and leave the area. Children should respect the dog's desire and not follow. They should also learn not to disturb her while she is sleeping.

Car Travel

Most Ridgebacks like car trips. They are easier if your dog does not get anxious, carsick, or unruly. Start teaching your puppy when she is young how to ride in the car. Do not let her bark, run among the seats, or hang her head out the window. A variety of harness restraints are available that allow your dog to ride safely and securely in the car. If your car is large enough, your dog can also safely travel in her crate.

Young children playing with puppies should always be supervised.

Take your puppy on short errands to get her used to riding in the car. If you occasionally schedule a stop at a park where she can play or let her out to visit an admirer, she will be even happier to go. Teach your puppy not to bolt from the car. She should learn to wait until you give the command to jump in or out. Leaving a hard chew bone when your puppy is alone in the car will give her something to do while she waits for your return. If your puppy does not ride in a crate, keep your initial absences from the car brief. You do not want her chewing the car's interior.

Be aware of outside temperatures when you leave your dog alone in the car. The temperature inside a car can become hot, even when the windows are open and the car is parked in the shade. The glass hatchbacks of some cars also cause the car to heat up rapidly. On cold, snowy days, some Ridgebacks might willingly wear a dog sweater while waiting in the car.

top: You must puppy-proof your home and yard to provide a safe environment for your Ridgeback puppy.

above: Training a puppy is demanding but will result in a well-mannered adult canine companion.

left: Puppies are playful and curious.

An adult Ridgeback obtained through a rescue organization can make a loyal companion.

An experienced breeder can assess a puppy's show potential, but cannot offer any guarantees on what the individual will be as an adult.

Ridgebacks are a relatively easy breed to housebreak, but keep several points in mind. Some puppies are easy to housebreak. They make no mistakes, and within a few days they stand by the door when they need to go outside. Others take longer. House-breaking can be more difficult to accomplish if you are at work all day.

A crate will make house-breaking your new puppy easier and more effective. By keeping your puppy in her crate when you cannot watch her, you help prevent accidents in the house. Use of a crate reduces housebreaking time to a minimum and avoids keeping the puppy and yourself under constant stress by continually correcting her for making mistakes.

Consistency

As with any type of training, consistency is the key. Puppies have four typical times they need to eliminate: when they first wake in the morning, immediately after eating each meal, about 15 minutes after playtime, and just before bedtime.

Develop a schedule for your puppy so she is taken out at these same times each day. Along with a regular elimination schedule, feeding your puppy at consistent times will make housebreaking easier.

When you wake up in the morning, the first thing you need to do is take your puppy outside. For the first week or two, you might need to carry your puppy to avoid the chance of an accident happening on the way outside. Give the *outside* command as you leave the house. Set her down in the same place each time. Do not leave her outside by herself. You must make sure that she does her business. Stand quietly and wait. Use a *bathroom* command such as *"Go pee,"* and praise her when she eliminates. Then take her back inside.

If she does not go in a few minutes, take her back inside. Do not let her stay outside to play. This helps her learn that the outdoors is for elimination. Keep the bathroom area clean of droppings. The smell of urine will encourage your puppy to use the spot.

Put her in her crate each evening to reduce the chance of accidents, but be sure she has eliminated before doing

Taking your puppy outside is the first thing you should do every morning.

HOUSEBREAKING

so. Taking your puppy outside late at night can help her sleep through the night. If your puppy wakes up whimpering, chances are she has to go outside.

Does the Puppy Need to Go?

When puppies need to urinate, they often stop and squat with little warning. To prevent accidents, use timing. How long was it since your puppy last went outside? If it has been more than a few hours, take her outside and praise her when she goes. When puppies need to defecate, their behavior changes. They suddenly stop playing and begin to sniff around. Some might circle around and around in preparation to eliminate. Keep a watchful eye out for these behaviors. If necessary, quickly scoop up your puppy and take her outside. Be alert; your puppy might stand by the door when she needs to go outside.

If you catch your puppy in the act of making a mistake, use a firm *"No,"* loud enough to startle, but do not yell at her. Do not get angry and scare your puppy. Pulling or pushing your puppy hurriedly out the door will not stop the puppy from going and will only frighten her.

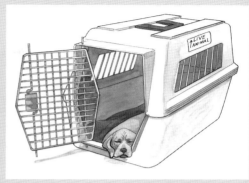

A crate is an essential piece of equipment for your Ridgeback and an important aid in successful housebreaking.

Pick up your puppy, take her outside, and give her bathroom command. Praise her for going outside, and then bring her back inside again.

If you discover a mistake your puppy already made, do not yell or push her nose into the mess. She will not understand. Such methods can derail the housebreaking process and create more problems. After you clean up the mess, use an odor-neutralizing product sold at pet stores. This will remove any scent that might attract your puppy to the same place.

PRACTICAL TRAINING

Carrying a lovable Ridgeback puppy into your house for the first time is exciting. His trusting eyes, large paws, and silky fur carry the promise of unlimited potential. Formal obedience training is the best insurance to help guarantee you and your Ridgeback a happy life together.

Why Train?

Puppies naturally love people, but they do not know how to live in people's homes or interact with people in an acceptable manner. A puppy does not know the rules and must be taught how to behave and what is right and wrong.

Training is how you communicate with your dog. It lets your Ridgeback know what is expected and will not break his spirit. Dogs who are trained are secure and confident because they know where they fit in a family's structure and in human society. Knowing what is and is not allowed enhances a dog's self-confidence. Training enables an undisciplined, obnoxious dog to learn acceptable ways to get attention. Dogs who are shy and insecure become more confident. Dominant dogs learn that you are the boss.

Keep training sessions short and interesting for adult Ridgebacks.

When most people get a puppy, they think it will be forever. However, the unexpected does happen, and for a variety of reasons people have to relinquish their dog. You, a rescue group, or a shelter will find your dog a new home more easily if he is trained, socialized, and well mannered. Because people sometimes give up their dogs due to bad behavior, the commitment to formal training can help prevent this possibility.

How to Train

The key to successful dog training is consistency. Dogs are creatures of habit, so train using the same commands for the same responses. Always praise for good behavior and never ignore lapses even once, only to reprimand for them at another time.

When to Begin Training

Begin training as soon as your puppy enters your home. As long as you are clear on what is and is not allowed, your puppy will learn quickly. A basic rule of dog training is that preventing problems is easier than fixing them. A puppy is just a baby and should not always be expected to be on his best behavior. Let him be a puppy, but direct and encourage behaviors that are desirable for an adult dog. Do not encourage behaviors that will be difficult to tolerate in an adult.

Short Sessions

Puppies have a short attention span, but long memories. Outside of class, keep your training sessions short, and integrate numerous short sessions into daily life. For example, tell your puppy to *"Sit"* before each meal. When working on a command, do not practice for so long that your puppy loses interest and is bored. Executing a command two to three times is often enough. Always end a training session on a positive note while your puppy is still interested and has performed a command well. Train your puppy both when he is behaving well and when he is ornery—obedience is not just limited to your puppy's good times. Work with your puppy to build his confidence and trust in your authority. As your puppy matures, training sessions can lengthen and incorporate more commands.

Your puppy will take some time to learn simple commands, such as *sit* and *stay*. Yet as he matures and the more you train your puppy, the faster he will learn to learn and the more easily you will be able to teach additional commands.

Your tone of voice should reflect your leadership role. Firmly give a command only once, and then, if necessary, enforce it. Avoid giving commands such as *"Come on, sit down."* Your commands should be clear and concise, and the puppy should have no doubt what you mean (i.e., *"sit"* or *"down"*). Use one-word commands. Do not whine, cajole, or plead, *"Please, come on, sit down."* This tone of voice can communicate distress to your dog since it sounds like whimpering; at the very least, it is not clear and forceful. Change the tone of your voice when you give a verbal correction. If your puppy still does not respond, issue the correction in a firmer, growling tone.

Timing: When to give praise or a correction is very important. In order for your puppy to associate his behavior with your response, your praise or correction must be given when his behavior is occurring (within three seconds!). Dogs do not have a human concept of time. Your dog will not remember that five minutes ago he was chewing on the leg of a chair. Therefore, he will not associate your anger with

Pack Structure

Your dog is a pack animal, and you are his wise and benevolent leader, never capricious or cruel. Obedience training in dogs operates on this premise. Like a good pack member, your dog will learn to take directions from you. You give your dog the rules and conditions to live by, which give him confidence about his position. Your Ridgeback should be a happy, lower-ranked member of your family pack who is willing to accept your commands and control as well as those of all other family members. You must act like a leader and enforce your role. For example, your dog must not only obey you, he must not rush out the door ahead of you, and he must relinquish a toy or bone to you when asked.

his previous actions. However, in response to your upset demeanor (even if you think you are not giving out any signals), he will lower his body and eyes and put back his ears. Dog owners interpret this submissive posture as guilt. However, most animal behaviorists agree—dogs do not feel guilt, spite, or other negative human emotions that are often attributed to them, most notably when they have been bad.

Aversion Tools

Sometimes a puppy is so thoroughly engaged in an activity, he appears not to hear the word *"No."* When *"No"* is not enough to dissuade your puppy from pulling on the curtains or gnawing on the leg of a chair, you can use an aversion tool. A variety of methods, including shake cans (soda cans filled with pennies or pebbles), small water pistols, whistles, or even loudly clapping your hands together, can be used as aversion tools. The goal is to break your puppy's concentration so that he stops what he is doing. Just as with the command *"No,"* when your puppy looks up, you must redirect him from the activity in which he was engaged and then praise him for doing right.

Timing is important. You must use the aversion method when your puppy is engaged in the undesired behavior, not after he has already stopped. Rather than searching for where you left a whistle or shake can, clapping your hands together often works best. Do not overuse an aversion tool. It is a method of last resort. Do not use it in a threatening manner. Its purpose is to startle, but not scare, your puppy so you can redirect him to an acceptable behavior.

TIP

Obedience Classes

Obedience classes provide a forum for training that is not easily replicated by an owner with a single puppy. Most Ridgeback puppies are capable of beginning formal obedience class when they are nine weeks old (provided the instructor requests proof that all canines are either vaccinated or on a vaccination schedule). In a class with older dogs, the puppies often learn the best. A solid foundation in basic obedience commands will make your puppy's rebellious adolescent stage easier.

Positive Reinforcement

Dogs can be effectively trained with either negative or positive reinforcement. The difference between the two methods is that dogs trained with positive reinforcement respond more enthusiastically, learn more quickly, and even become more creative in trying to figure out what you want. Positive reinforcement uses praise, such as a small tidbit of food or your voice, and correction, not punishment, to achieve the desired behavior. Because Ridgebacks love food, they are very easy to motivate with food treats. A chance to play games is also an effective reward for some dogs, especially when your Ridgeback's attention wanes.

The Leader

You must take the leadership role with your Ridgeback. If you do not, your Ridgeback will have you living according to his terms, not

Keeping your Ridgeback's attention is important whenever you share a training session.

Working with your dog so that he learns new skills and watching him perform is rewarding.

Dogs that do well in obedience competitions obey consistently and enjoy working with their owners.

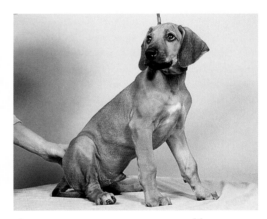

As your puppy grows, you can add new commands to teach him.

yours. This will create a bad situation for all when your puppy becomes full grown. As your puppy matures and, in particular, when an adolescent, he will occasionally try to challenge your authority. You must not ignore his challenges. To many people, these challenges can be subtle, but most start with the ignored command.

Never give your dog a command that you are not prepared or able to enforce. This means you do not "lazily" request your dog to sit and ignore his disobedience when he does not comply. If you are not going to follow through, do not give your puppy a command.

You are more likely to follow through in a structured setting, such as obedience class or when you are practicing your puppy's lessons, and less likely at home when you are busy and distracted. This is when it matters most, because this is how your puppy will share your home. Many Ridgebacks are savvy to home life and learn there are situations when you are unlikely to correct them, such as when you are talking on the phone or eating dinner. To prevent your dog from becoming obnoxious, excuse yourself for a moment and rectify the situation.

As your puppy's leader, you must be consistent and persistent and enforce your commands and rules. Doing so can be hard work but is ultimately worth it. You must be alert and pay attention to your puppy, even when you are tired or your puppy's misbehavior is cute. Sometimes it will seem easier to ignore half-bad behavior than to correct it. However, if you give your puppy an inch, it can sometimes lead to a mile. You must have the emotional fortitude to enforce boundaries. Arbitrarily enforcing rules will confuse your puppy and can lead to his challenging your authority.

Training Equipment

A flat-buckle collar is usually sufficient for your puppy's first six months of training. When he reaches his adolescent stage and becomes a bit rebellious, you should then purchase a chain or nylon choke collar. Be careful when using the choke collar. A Ridgeback does not have thick fur to protect his throat against abuse. A choke collar works with a quick pop,

Successful house-training requires taking your puppy outside on a regular schedule.

not by yanking and spinning your puppy around or by sustained pulling. In addition to a 6-foot (1.8-m) leash, a retractable leash or drag line (at least 20 feet [6.1 m] long) is

Continual exposure to new people, activities, and environments will help your Ridgeback puppy grow into a confident dog that can adapt to a variety of situations.

A Trainer's Role

1. Teach you *how* to train your puppy or dog without you losing your patience or resorting to aggressive threats or punishment

2. Discover any problems in your techniques so that you can be more effective

3. Recognize behaviors in your puppy that you otherwise would not, such as dominant or fearful tendencies

4. Teach you to establish yourself as your dog's master

5. Help you adhere to a regular training schedule

6. Illustrate *how* to train your puppy for each specific command

needed. These longer leads help you to practice and enforce obedience commands when your puppy is further away from you.

Family Members

All family members should take turns attending the puppy's obedience classes, including children who are of at least elementary school age. This will help the whole family use consistent training methods and commands. Family members who do not help to train the puppy often issue a variety of conflicting and confusing instructions. The puppy becomes stressed and ends up ignoring everyone but the person who trained him.

Finding a Trainer

Before you sign up with any trainer, observe some classes. Avoid a trainer whose class seems chaotic and out of control. Trainers that use harsh or physical treatment should also be avoided. You should never hit your Ridgeback.

This breed is highly sensitive. Anger, force, or physical punishment can make them shy and unwilling to work with you. Do not develop an adversarial relationship with your Ridgeback. If you find yourself growing frustrated and angry when practicing a lesson, stop the training session and return to it only when your emotions are under control.

Basic Obedience Commands

Sit, down, stay, come, and *heel* are the five simple obedience commands that every dog needs to know. If you go on to advanced training, you will teach your dog to respond to hand signals and additional commands.

Always train your puppy on a leash so that you have control over him. Without a leash, you have no way of enforcing your commands, and your Ridgeback puppy might get bored and walk away or realize that he does not have to listen to you. The only way a puppy learns to obey commands is to realize that once given, commands must be obeyed. Give a command only once before enforcing it. You want your Ridgeback to respond to *"Stay,"* not to *"Stay, Stay, Stay."* Once your puppy responds reflexively to your commands in a variety of situations and circumstances, then you can begin to practice each command off leash.

Undoubtedly, the instructor for the obedience class in which you enroll your puppy will have a preferred method for teaching the basic commands. However, in some areas, classes are not available or they do not accept puppies younger than a certain age, such as six months. Your puppy is extremely receptive to learning between seven and twelve weeks of age; do not waste this time just because no class is available. The following methods of teaching the basic commands work well. Follow up with additional commands found in training books and from local dog clubs.

Proper use of food treats is important. When first learning a command, immediately praise and give a food treat when your puppy has done what you wanted. Once your puppy has learned a command, you will switch and randomly reward him with the treat or praise. Your puppy will perform his best if he does not know when to expect a treat. As his repertoire of commands increases, you will reward him with a food treat only for learning new commands. Eventually, you will not use food treats at all. Verbally praise your puppy according to his performance. Do not reward him the same for different responses. Be effusive when he responds quickly and enthusiastically. When his response is weaker, make him work harder to get your attention or a positive response.

The Command "No"

Inevitably, your puppy will learn the command *"No!"* shortly after he comes into your home. Do not frighten your puppy into learning this command. Just say it loudly enough for the puppy to hear, and then give him something else to do or put him out of harm's way. Avoid overusing this command; your puppy should not think his name ends or begins with *"No."* If you see your puppy heading toward mischief, head him off and give him something acceptable to do.

Release Command

Of absolute importance is a *release* command. This command lets your puppy know that he can break the previous command and resume doing what he wants. Many owners make the mistake of telling their dog to sit or lie down and then they forget about their dog. Eventually the dog gets up and moves. Sometimes the owner yells at the dog for moving, but other times the owner ignores the dog. This inconsistency confuses the dog.

Therefore, never give a command without also knowing that you want your dog to break it only when you release him. For example, when you command your puppy to sit, you will let him know he can get up from the *sit* when you give the *release* command. If at first your puppy does not seem to understand the *release* command, get him excited and he will break his position.

The word "OK" is not the best choice for a *release* command because it is often used in everyday conversation. If your dog is sitting at your side while you are talking to someone and you use the word "OK" in the conversation, your dog will probably break his *sit*. If you are in a busy location and your dog is not on a leash, this could have bad consequences. For this reason, many trainers prefer *"Release!"* or *"Break!"*

Other Useful Commands

Leave it: Teach your puppy this command when he is in the *down-stay* position. Place several food treats on the ground just out of the puppy's reach and say *"Leave it."* Stand on the leash should he try to strain forward. Wait a minute and then say *"Good leave it,"* and reward him with a different treat. This command is useful for teaching your puppy to leave garbage, animal droppings, and even some people alone.

Give usually means your puppy delivers and places an object in his mouth into your hand.

Practice *give* with your puppy's bones and toys. As the leader, you have the right to take away your puppy's toys or chews. Calmly and gently say *"Give,"* and firmly take away the object. Do not let your puppy grab it back. Praise your puppy, and then give him back his toy or bone. Incorporating play, not a food treat, will reward your puppy for giving you the object.

The command drop it means your puppy drops whatever he has in his mouth onto the ground. Teach your puppy this command by gently opening his mouth so he drops the object. Say *"Drop it,"* and then praise him. This is useful when your puppy has something disgusting like a dead animal or dropping in his mouth and you do not want to touch it.

Dog shows are a fun place to socialize with other people who love Ridgebacks.

Out: This command is useful if you want your puppy to stay out of a certain room. Your tone of voice, stance, and demeanor should indicate what you want.

Socialization

Socialization occurs when you expose your puppy to new environments, such as parks, shops, noisy school yards, and friends' homes, and you introduce him to as many new people as possible of all ages and sizes. As long as he is calm and happy, socialization helps your puppy learn to get along with others and provides your puppy with positive experiences so he does not become shy or fearful. Socialization will help to prevent potential future problems and is as important for your Ridgeback as basic obedience training. The peak socialization opportunity ends around 12 weeks of age, so be sure to perform this exercise well before that age.

Check with your veterinarian as to the safest age to take your puppy to new places. Because of the risk of infection to a puppy who has not completed his vaccinations, limit your puppy's exposure to other dogs and avoid areas where dogs concentrate (e.g., dog parks). Do let him meet friendly dogs who have current vaccinations.

You should continue to socialize your puppy as he grows and matures. Keep your puppy on a leash during these excursions for safety and control. Make your excursions positive experiences. Reassure your puppy if he becomes scared, but do so with happy, bold words.

Even if you do not have children, socializing your puppy with children is very important. Life is full of unpredictable changes; socializing

A well-socialized Ridgeback is calm and reliable in a wide variety of situations.

your puppy with children can better prepare you and your dog to meet these changes. If you do not have children, take your puppy to a park on the weekend. Let him smell, see, and hear children running and playing. Parents will usually bring over their children to visit, or a child might ask if he or she can pet your puppy. It is best if your puppy already knows how to sit so that he is under control. Since a Ridgeback puppy is irresistible, have some small pieces of dog biscuit a child can offer to your puppy, who is sitting. Be prepared to correct the puppy if he tries to jump or get unruly. Because young puppies still have sharp teeth and might grab, the child can offer the treat on a flat hand. Children and adults are usually receptive and patient if you tell them your puppy is in training and is learning how to behave properly.

Troubleshooting

Dogs live in the present, meaning you can correct only behavior you see. This might require you to be hypervigilant, or you can bait your puppy by setting up a situation to help him learn what he can and cannot do. For example, correcting your puppy for chewing shoes after they are already shredded is less effective than catching him in the act. Some puppies may stop chewing on their own, but others might still view shoes as tasty toys. Help your puppy learn what he cannot chew by leaving the shoes where he can find them while you are watching. When he tries to take a shoe, correct him, and then give him an appropriate toy in place of the shoe. This tactic is effective with many problem behaviors, although you might have to reinforce the lesson several times.

Sit

Many Ridgeback puppies quickly learn this command after only a few repetitions. Give the command *"Sit,"* and gently push down on your puppy's hindquarters until he sits. Immediately praise him. Alternatively, show him a treat, then raise the treat above his head so that he naturally moves into the sitting position. As he does this, say *"Sit"* and give the treat. Have him sit for a few seconds, then give your *release* command so he can get up. When you have his attention again, repeat the lesson. If your puppy tries to get up before the *release* command, pull up on the leash so he sits again or, if necessary, push down on his hindquarters. Praise, then release him.

Down

Next you can teach *down*. First have your puppy sit. Then show him a treat, and move the treat down and forward until the treat is in front of his paws. The puppy should move into the *down* position. As he does this, say *"Down,"* and reward him. If necessary, gently push down on his shoulders. He can get back up after you give the *release* command. Some puppies do not like the *down* command because it puts them in a subordinate position.

Stay

Next you will teach the command *"Stay"* while your puppy is in the *down* position. Command your puppy *"Down,"* then put your palm forward, in front of his face, and say *"Stay."* Stand up and step back a few paces. Move slowly and wait a few seconds before returning to your puppy. Put your foot on the leash so your puppy cannot jump up when you get closer. Praise your puppy for staying, give him a treat, and then release him.

If your puppy gets up before you release him, put him back in the *down* position without scolding and start again. Gradually increase the distance you go from your puppy. After he stays with you standing in front of him, slowly circle around him. Hold the leash, and let it slide through your hand so you can exert pressure should your puppy try to get up. An instructor is useful when you are teaching *stay* and increasing your distance from your puppy. If your puppy tries to follow you, the instructor can quickly correct him. (The puppy might perceive you running back to correct him as a reward for breaking his *stay*.) Aim to teach your puppy to stay when you are out of his sight and for up to ten minutes. Proceed slowly and very gradually, though.

Come

Come means your dog quickly comes directly to you and looks at you, waiting for

Participating in a training class is essential for you and your Rhodesian Ridgeback.

COMMANDS

further instruction. This is an essential command that can save your dog's life and save you from yelling yourself hoarse. It is very important that when you teach this command you are able to enforce it. When starting a training program, do not use *come* if you cannot make your puppy respond. Give the command only if you have a 6-foot (1.8-m) or a retractable leash attached to your puppy. Give the command only once. If your puppy does not pay attention, give the leash a quick pop. Open your arms, bend down, be enthusiastic, and your puppy will respond. Lavishly praise or give a treat to your puppy for coming when called, then release and repeat the exercise.

A few caveats: Start training from short distances (e.g., 5 feet [1.5 m]) and progress to longer distances using the retractable leash or drag line. Practice the command in a variety of situations. Once your puppy consistently responds to the command when on leash, practice training off leash. Do not run after your puppy if he ignores you; instead call his name and slowly jog away (your puppy cannot resist the invitation to pursue you). Call him only when there is a high likelihood that he will respond (i.e., he is not doing something more interesting). Finally, no matter how frustrated you get, never yell at him for eventually coming.

Many times when people have their dog off leash and they want the dog to range closer to them, they give the command *"Come."* The dog proceeds toward them but then veers away or stops short of the owner. Since the owner wanted the dog in closer, which is what the dog did, they ignore the fact that the dog did not come to them. Eventually, the command *come* erodes into *"Come closer to me, but you don't have to come to me."* To prevent this, use another command, such as *"Yip," "Here,"* or a unique whistle, when you want your dog to range in closer to you.

Even a well-trained Ridgeback is likely to succumb to this kind of temptation.

Save *come* for when you mean it and can practice how it should be performed.

Heel

When you are walking your 85-pound (38.6-kg) Ridgeback on a leash, he is supposed to keep pace with you, not charge ahead, dragging you along. Teaching the *heel* command is easiest when your dog is a puppy. *Heel* is the command you will use to teach your puppy to walk on a loose leash, without pulling. You must first train your puppy to line up on your left side. While standing in front of your puppy, use a food treat to move him behind your back and into a sitting position at your left side. Give the command *"Line up"* and reward him.

From this position, you will purposely move forward with your left leg and give the command *"Heel."* If your puppy bolts ahead of you, do a 180-degree turn and move in the opposite direction. Enough surprise turns will teach him that you are the leader and he has to pay attention and follow you. For best results, continue to practice this as your puppy grows and develops, and eventually train in different locations.

CARING FOR THE ADULT

Behavior problems are one of the main reasons people give up their dogs. You can unintentionally cultivate behavior problems in your dog by choosing the path of least resistance. Unconditionally accepting whatever behavior your dog shows and making excuses for it will lead to problems.

Behavior Problems

Dogs are creatures of habit and adapt best to clear rules. Do not give your canine mixed messages. She is either allowed on the bed and furniture or she is not. Like people, dogs do not adapt as willingly or as well to rules that become more restrictive. Decide early what furniture, if any, your Ridgeback will share with you. Be vigilant with the visitors who allow your dog to jump on them when you are actively working to teach her not to jump.

Dogs sometimes develop problem behaviors in response to changes in their owner's life. Some of the reasons for the changes might be difficult to detect. If your dog begins to display troubling behaviors, an animal behaviorist can help to find the cause and develop a training program to eliminate the behavior. Most veterinarians or

Time for off-leash play sessions is essential for a Rhodesian Ridgeback's fitness and happiness.

reputable breeders can recommend one. Manufacturers have also developed a variety of products that can assist your efforts to modify unwanted behavior such as barking or sneaking on furniture.

Barking

Although not known as excessive barkers, a Ridgeback given inadequate exercise and attention can develop into a nuisance barker who barks because she is lonely and bored. If you are not home during the day to correct this behavior, it can develop into a problem. Several antibarking devices, such as collars that squirt citronella oil or administer a small shock, can be used to help stop barking. However, the underlying reasons for the barking (e.g., boredom) must be addressed.

Jumping

Friendly dogs and puppies jump up on people as a form of greeting, especially when they are happy and excited. However, a dog who jumps can be annoying or dangerous. You can use several methods to prevent or correct this problem. Crouch down when greeting your puppy so she does not have to jump. Calmly greet your puppy; do not get excited upon seeing her. Redirect your puppy's enthusiasm by distracting her with something else, such as tossing one of her toys. Because jumping up is self-rewarding, teach your puppy that jumping will be ignored. If she jumps on you, step back or turn aside so she cannot make contact, and ignore her until all four feet are on the ground. When your puppy jumps, firmly state *"No!"* Give the command *"Off!"* followed by the command *"Sit."* When she complies, then visit and praise. If necessary, holding and squeezing your dog's paws for one or two minutes while looking away is effective. Kneeing a dog in the chest can cause serious internal injuries and is not recommended.

Dominance Behavior

Your dog should never exhibit aggressive behavior, such as growling at you, a family member, or a friend. If your dog growls when asked to get off the couch or bed or when a person wants to join her on the couch or bed, you have a problem. Dominance aggression occurs in situations where the dog believes she is in charge. It is typically directed at people who the dog does not consider her equal. Guarding behavior of a food dish, bone, or toy should also not be tolerated. Ridgebacks are not typically possessive of objects. Nonetheless, while still a puppy, they should be taught to relinquish objects when asked and not to display guarding behavior. Obedience training as early as possible can help curb any tendencies toward dominance behavior. If your dog exhibits dominance aggression, you will need the help of a professional trainer.

Spaying and Neutering

Spaying refers to removal of the female dog's ovaries and uterus. The male dog is neutered, which refers to the removal of the male's testicles. You should fix your dog. After this procedure, your dog's activity level and personality will not change.

Female dogs who are spayed before their first heat cycle, which can occur between 7 to 24 months of age, have a lesser risk of developing mammary cancer. A female dog's three-week heat cycle is messy. Although she will try to keep herself clean, her efforts are usually not sufficient to keep the bloody discharge from dirtying carpets and any furniture she is allowed on. Additionally, protecting a willing female in heat from determined males is extremely difficult.

Male dogs are not usually neutered until they are about one year old. Neutering can decrease a male's dominance aggression toward other unneutered males. Because of the high incidence of reproductive disorders in older dogs, most veterinarians recommend neutering dogs by their eighth birthday, as practiced by most breeders.

Playthings for Adults

Your dog will continue to play with and enjoy the same types of toys she had as a puppy, although they might need to be larger in size. Bones are necessary to keep your dog's gums and teeth healthy and clean, and to provide a healthy outlet for her need to chew. However, now that she is an adult, you might notice that she quickly devours her rawhide bones. Some Ridgebacks are voracious chewers and gulp down chunks of hooves or bolt pieces of rawhide. This can cause intestinal upset and blockages, which might even require surgical removal. If your dog is of this type, avoid offering cow hooves and rawhide chews. Cow hooves are also very hard and have been known to fracture teeth in some dogs. Supervise your dog when she chews to determine if there is a problem. Other chewing options include nylabones or large, marrow bones. Some of the smoked bones are crumbly and too easily consumed, also causing problems. Do not give your dog any small bones, which usually include any from your family's dinner.

Grooming

Brushing: Ridgebacks are fondly referred to as wash-and-wear-dogs. Their short smooth coat is easy to care for and does not require special brushing. A rubber brush or hound glove is ideal to help remove loose hair. Once or twice a week is sufficient to remove debris, dirt, and hair. A chamois leather cloth will give the coat a smooth shine. Mud is easily brushed off once it is dry.

All dogs shed, although compared with many breeds a Ridgeback's shedding is less noticeable. Their short fine hairs do not readily stick to clothes or furniture but usually just fall to the floor. If allowed on furniture, a fine dusting of hair might be left behind. Ridgebacks shed

Although a variety of brushes are sold, the Ridgeback's short coat is best groomed with a rubber brush or hound glove.

most obviously in the spring. Because they do not have a thick undercoat, molting is easily dealt with by a quick brushing every few days.

Bathing: Ridgebacks seldom need a bath and do not often smell pungent. Some collars retain a strong doggy smell, and a new collar rather than a bath might be necessary. Otherwise, it is time for a bath if you pet your dog and your hands become coated with a film of dirt. Ridgebacks do not like baths. Giving your dog an occasional bath while she is still young will get her used to the experience.

It is often easier to bathe your dog outside using a hose that attaches to your inside faucet. Use warm water. Be careful not to get shampoo in your dog's eyes or ears, which can cause irritation, and to rinse thoroughly to avoid dandruff. Your dog can dry in the warm sun, but if it is cool outside, rub your dog dry with a towel and keep her inside and out of drafts.

Nails: You might be able to avoid cutting your puppy's nails. However, an adult Ridgeback's nails can grow relatively quickly, and you will eventually need to cut them.

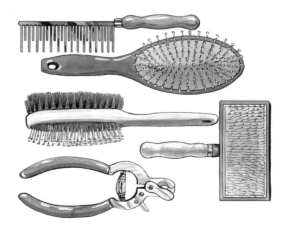

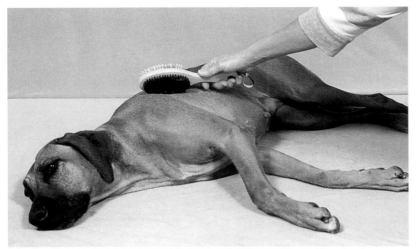

Regular grooming will help you monitor your Ridgeback's health and condition and learn what is normal for him.

Start trimming your puppy's nails while he is still young to get him used to the procedure.

The Rhodesian Ridgeback is familiarly known as a "wash-and-wear-dog," and for good reason. Grooming requirements for this naturally attractive breed are simple.

A puppy will mouth anything, so make sure there are no poisonous plants in your backyard.

Introduce your Ridgeback puppy to as many experiences as possible.

Although the breed originated in Africa, Rhodesian Ridgebacks usually enjoy snow.

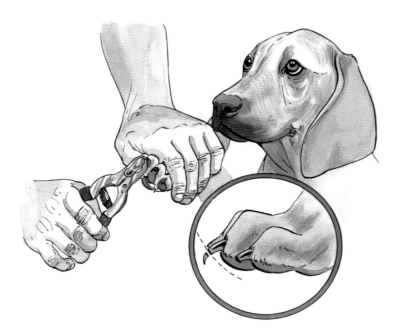

Slowly trim your Ridgeback's nails to avoid cutting the quick.

Unless regularly exercised on rough surfaces, the nails on the adult's front feet will not wear down by themselves. Because Ridgebacks push off with their hind feet when running, the nails on the back feet tend to be regularly worn down.

If you can hear your dog's nails click against a hard floor or if the nails touch the floor surface, they are probably too long and should be trimmed. Overgrown nails can snag and tear. A torn nail is painful and can become infected. Markedly overgrown nails can cause a dog to walk incorrectly and even cause joint stress because the dog walks on the back half of her paws. A nail's quick will grow out as the nail lengthens. If you wait too long between periods of nail cutting, you will have to cut the tips back gradually over a period of days and weeks to return the nails to a healthy length. Most

Ridgebacks have their dewclaws removed. Dewclaws are functionless claws on the inside of the front feet that do not reach the ground when walking. If your dog still has her dewclaws, you must also trim them regularly.

Use dog nail clippers to cut the nail below the quick, which is the portion that contains the nails' blood supply and nerves. If your dog's nails are light colored, you can see the dark line of quick. Shining a flashlight at the nail will sometimes help to illuminate the quick. You can also have your dog lie on her back and examine the nails from underneath to determine where the quick is located.

By trimming off small portions at a time rather than making one large cut, you are less likely to cut the quick accidentally. If you do draw blood, apply pressure with a wet cloth for three to five minutes to stop the bleeding. You can also apply a commercial clotting powder to the end of the nail to stop the bleeding.

For an animal that runs barefoot with ease over a variety of surfaces, a dog can be amazingly ticklish about having her feet handled. Practice touching, holding, and examining your puppy's feet so that she will learn not to mind having her feet handled.

Dental care: Dogs can suffer from periodontal disease, abscesses, and tooth decay and loss. To prevent these conditions, a dog's teeth need dental care. Teeth covered with tartar and inflamed gums can cause more than bad breath; the bacteria can travel from infected teeth and gums to the dog's heart and kidneys, causing a serious infection in these organs. Bones, such as rawhides and nylabones, and hard crunchy foods can help prevent tartar from accumulating on your dog's teeth.

You can remove tartar with a variety of products, including a soft toothbrush and dog toothpaste, tooth scalers and scrapers, and dental cleaning wipes. Brushing your dog's teeth at least once a week with a soft toothbrush and dog toothpaste will help keep them free of plaque and tartar. Scalers and scrapers can be used less often. Always scrape away from the dog's gum line. These sharp tools can cut your dog if used incorrectly.

Because cleaning at the gum line is difficult, a professional cleaning is eventually necessary. The results will help keep your dog's teeth strong and healthy and keep her breath from smelling foul.

Ear care: Many Ridgebacks seldom need to have their ears cleaned, but some individuals produce a lot of wax or frequent dirty or dusty areas. Either way, you should make it a habit to check your dog's ears every week or so. Keeping the ears clean of debris will help prevent them from becoming smelly and possibly infected. For many dogs, wiping the outer part clean with cotton balls will suffice. Carefully use a cotton swab to remove any wax or debris farther down the ear. Do not allow the swab to enter the ear canal, which is beyond the area you can easily see. Doing so can seriously injure your dog's ear.

Ears that are continually dirty could indicate an infection or an infestation with ear mites, which are transmitted from other dogs. If your dog's ears smell bad, look irritated, or have a discharge, she needs to be examined by a veterinarian.

Usually, if your dog gets something in her ear, such as a grass seed, she will shake or scratch her head or carry her head at a tilt. If you cannot see anything in your dog's ear, you must take her to a veterinarian.

FEEDING

Good nutrition is a key factor in promoting a long and healthy life for your dog. Dogs need a balanced and nutritious diet that includes the appropriate amounts of protein, carbohydrates, fats, vitamins, and minerals.

Understanding Nutrition

The items that compose a particular dog food are stated in the product's ingredients list and are listed in descending order by weight. The first three to five items on an ingredient list make up most of the food.

On every bag or can of dog food is a guaranteed analysis, which tells you what amount of protein, fat, fiber, and moisture are in the food. The protein and fat contents are stated as minimums, while the fiber and moisture contents are stated as maximums. The word *crude*, which precedes each measure, refers to laboratory analysis rather than digestibility.

Types of Food

Commercial dog food is available in two basic forms: dry and canned. Nutritionally complete and balanced dry food is the most

A truly well-nourished dog is owned by a person who understands a dog's food needs and what foods will provide them.

economical way to feed your dog. Because of its low moisture content, dry food is usually more concentrated. The hard, abrasive surface of dry food helps to decrease the accumulation of dental tartar on the teeth of some dogs. Compared with dry foods, canned food is more expensive per pound. Some canned foods are nutritionally complete, while others are designed as a supplemental gravy to increase a dry food's palatability. Many dogs relish canned food's taste and consistency. Your Ridgeback will be delighted if you add some canned food to his regular kibble at dinner time.

Life Stage and Specialty Diets

A dog's nutritional requirements change as he grows from a puppy into an adult and change again as he ages. Many dog food manufacturers have developed different types of foods to meet these changing nutritional needs. Life stage foods are more precisely formulated than a one-size-fits-all approach and usually incorporate the latest research findings.

Feeding these types of foods can best meet your dog's nutritional needs.

Foods for growing puppies contain more protein and fat than foods for adult dogs. In general, Ridgeback puppies can be fed the puppy food for their first year and then changed to an adult food. Excessive amounts of protein can cause muscles and other soft tissue to develop more quickly than the dog's bones and skeletal structure. Many experts believe that this can predispose large-breed dogs to conditions such as hip dysplasia. In response to these concerns, many manufacturers now offer foods designed specifically for large-breed puppies.

Senior: Once your Ridgeback is seven years old, he should be switched to one of the senior diets that are available. These foods are lower in protein, fat, and calories and are designed to meet the nutritional needs of older dogs.

Specialty diets are made for certain conditions. They include high-calorie foods for active and working dogs, sometimes called performance foods, and lower-calorie foods for overweight dogs. Prescription diets are formulated to manage different medical conditions. They are prescribed by veterinarians and are available only through your veterinarian. Other food manufacturers include a category of food supplements called nutraceuticals in their foods. Examples include glucosamine and chondroitin, which are thought to maintain and promote joint health. Scientific testing of some of these substances is only beginning.

Choosing a Food

Whatever brand of food you choose to feed, it should state that it provides an adequate diet according to the Association of American Feed Control Officers (AAFCO). Foods that meet AAFCO standards state on their package that the food provides complete and balanced nutrition either for all life stages (growth, reproduction, lactation, and adult dogs who are not pregnant) or for one or more life stages (such as growth and maintenance of dogs).

Even among the brands of dog food that do meet AAFCO standards, there is tremendous variation. Dog food can be classified into three categories: premium foods, grocery store brands, and generic brands, all of which might state they meet AAFCO standards. The best choice to feed your Ridgeback is a premium brand of dog food. Premium foods are the most expensive choice. The ingredients that make up premium products are typically more expensive, such as higher-quality animal protein and natural preservatives, such as vitamins C and E. The first ingredient in premium foods is usually an animal-based protein such as chicken. Premium foods can also vary in the quality of their ingredients. Some premium food manufacturers use human-grade ingredients, which are ingredients fit for human consumption. Premium food manufacturers use consistent ingredients blended to fixed formulas so the food is always the same. Dogs with sensitive digestive systems do best on premium foods.

Because the higher-quality ingredients in a premium food are more digestible per serving, your dog will not need to eat as much as a food with poorer-quality sources of nutrients. Dogs fed foods based primarily on grains, such as ground corn and corn gluten meal, usually need to eat more per pound of body weight and, consequently, produce larger and more numerous stools. Dogs who are fed premium foods appear healthier, with more lustrous coats, better skin condition, and fewer digestive problems.

Premium dog foods are sold at pet stores, veterinarian offices, and feed stores. A few brands are sold at grocery stores. Buy only one month's supply of food at a time, and buy the food from a busy store whose inventory is constantly turned over.

Although feeding a generic brand may seem cheaper, your dog would need to eat three to four times as much of a generic food compared with a premium food to provide proper nutrition. These foods cost less per pound, but they consist of lower-quality ingredients and are less likely to provide optimal nutrition. A dog fed a poor-quality diet may have a dull, coarse coat and be lethargic.

The main criterion that you should use to judge a food is your dog's response to it. After four to eight weeks of eating the food, how does your dog look? Is his fur dry or glossy? Is his skin flaky or soft and supple? Does he constantly scratch himself even if he has no fleas? Does he have a good appetite and firm stools? Does he have gas? Consider switching brands if your dog's coat does not look shiny, his skin is dry, or the food appears to cause persistent gas. If you change your dog's food, you should do so over a period of a week, gradually mixing the new food in with the old. Although some dogs can tolerate an abrupt change, others will experience a digestive upset, such as diarrhea.

Feeding a Puppy

Your breeder can tell you how much food to begin feeding your puppy. Ridgeback puppies between two and three months old should be fed three to four equal-sized meals a day. Feed only two or three meals a day after your puppy is three months old. Puppies older than five months should be fed twice a day, once in the morning and once in the evening. As your puppy grows, the amount of food you feed him should be gradually increased. If your puppy quickly finishes each meal, he might need a little more. If he leaves food in his dish after each feeding time, you are probably feeding too much.

Ideally, you should feed your puppy his meals at the same time every day. This will help you housebreak him because puppies eliminate shortly after eating. After every meal, you should take your puppy outside to do his business. Scheduled mealtimes will work only if you are home during the day. If you work during the day, the alternative method is to free feed your puppy. Free-fed puppies have access to dry food at all times. Puppies that are free-fed rarely overeat and become fat. A growing puppy should have a shiny coat and his ribs should show slightly. By one year of age, your Ridgeback's growth and development will slow down, and you can then switch him to an adult food and probably decrease the amount you feed him.

Feeding an Adult

The amount of food your dog will need to eat is affected by numerous factors. Active dogs need more food than less active dogs. The weather can affect how much food your dog eats. Just as people's appetites increase during cold weather, so might your dog's. If you take your dog for a long cross-country ski trip in snowy weather, you might observe that he has a ravenous appetite upon your return home. Just as people prefer light food during hot summer weather, you might notice that your dog's appetite decreases somewhat.

A growing puppy requires a high-quality food.

Feeding a premium diet will provide your dog with all the nutrients he needs to look and perform at his best.

Compared with unaltered dogs, fixed dogs often have a slower metabolism. Many dogs are altered shortly before or after they reach puberty, a time when their growth has slowed anyway, and they do not need to eat as much

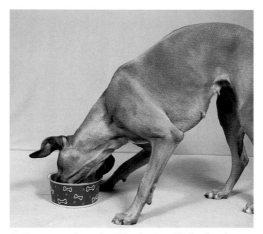

Like many breeds, Rhodesian Ridgebacks are usually enthusiastic eaters.

food as when they were growing puppies. Once your dog is spayed or neutered, carefully monitor your pet's weight to determine whether you need to adjust the amount of food you feed.

Offering food for only 15 minutes at each mealtime can help you to adjust the quantity you feed. If your dog does not eat his food, he might not be hungry. Try offering his meal at a later time. However, if your dog loses his appetite, especially for several days, he might be sick and should be taken to a veterinarian.

Adult Ridgebacks should have two meals a day. This will help your dog maintain a consistent energy level. Moreover, meal time is often the highlight of a dog's day; feeding him in the morning and in the evening can make the day more interesting for your dog. More importantly, Ridgebacks are potentially subject to bloat, which is an emergency medical condition described in detail in the health section. Feeding more than one meal a day helps to reduce the risk for this condition. Because of the potential for bloat, do not feed your dog a large meal and then take him out to exercise right away.

Feeding Etiquette

Dogs like schedules and do best when fed around the same time each day. Some dogs prefer to eat their meal in a quiet part of the house; others are not bothered by a lot of activity. Some dogs become protective of their food dish and the area in which they are fed. A dog must not growl or lunge at a person or child who walks by or up to the dog while he is eating. Ridgebacks are family-oriented dogs and rarely exhibit such tendencies.

Nonetheless, you should teach your Ridgeback manners at his mealtime. Your dog should sit and stay for his meal and eat only when released. Hand feeding your puppy some of his food during his mealtimes can help prevent food-guarding behavior from developing. Consult with a dog trainer if your puppy or adult dog shows aggressive behavior when fed.

Drinking Water

Make sure that your Ridgeback always has clean, fresh water. If your dog spends time both indoors and out, he should have water bowls in both locations. If needed, heated water bowls are sold for outside use, which prevent water from freezing. A Lixit (sold in pet stores) can be attached to an outside faucet and provides a constant supply of clean drinking water. Water bowls need to be washed at least every few days. A slime can coat the bowls, which will not be removed by simply emptying and refilling with water.

Adjust the amount you feed according to your dog's activity level.

When viewed from above, your Ridgeback should have an hourglass figure with a waist.

Food and Water Dishes

Dog dishes are available in stainless steel, heavy-duty ceramic, lightweight plastic, and hard rubber. The most important criterion is that the dishes are easy for you to wash and clean. Harmful bacteria and fungi can grow in bowls if they are not regularly cleaned. Because many people do not like adding to their workload, choosing a dish that can be washed in a dishwasher makes sense.

Table Scraps and Treats

Many people are adamantly against feeding a dog any kind of human food. Others enjoy sharing table scraps with their dog. As long as table scraps do not comprise more than 10 percent of your dog's diet, they are unlikely to cause any problems. However, when table scraps regularly comprise more than 25 percent of your dog's diet, problems such as obesity and imbalanced nutrition can occur.

Many people object to feeding scraps because they believe it encourages their

dog to beg. However, if the dog is not fed directly from the table and is kept out of the dining area during meals, begging should not be a problem. Some types of table scraps can cause digestive upset in sensitive dogs, resulting in flatulence (gas) or diarrhea. (Because of this possibility, do not feed your puppy any table scraps until after he is housebroken.) High-fat foods, such as French fries and potato chips, are particularly likely to cause such problems. Use good judgment if you choose to feed your Ridgeback leftovers.

Dogs like sweets such as chocolate. However, chocolate contains theobromine, which is toxic to dogs in large amounts. Chocolate can cause urinary incontinence, seizures, and death. Do not feed your dog chocolate, and be sure to keep any out of your resourceful Ridgeback's reach.

Other Edibles

Dogs are scavengers and will eat an amazing variety of disgusting things, including other animals' droppings. If you have a cat, be sure to place his litter box so that your Ridgeback cannot snack on the contents. This tendency is a good reason to teach your Ridgeback the command *"Drop it."* Doing so ideally prevents you from having to reach into your dog's mouth to take away a repulsive item. Also be sure to place your cat's food where your Ridgeback cannot get to it. Not only is it expensive to feed cat food to your dog, cat food is unhealthy for dogs because of the high protein levels.

Some Ridgebacks will readily raid garbage cans for repugnant refuse. Eating garbage

Choose food and water dishes that are easy to keep clean.

can cause potentially dangerous results, including intestinal blockages that require emergency surgery. Keep kitchen and bathroom trash cans out of your Ridgeback's reach. Ridgebacks are clever and some can learn to open cabinet doors and the refrigerator. If your dog can open cabinets, install additional latches to keep your dog safe. Full-grown Ridgebacks are tall. They can easily reach kitchen counters. Be careful not to leave items defrosting on the countertop or potentially hazardous items, such as a box of chocolates, within your dog's reach.

Bones

Like most dogs, Ridgebacks enjoy chewing bones. Gnawing on bones massages a dog's gums and helps to clean his teeth by scraping off tartar and other debris. However, never feed your dog any kind of bone from your leftover meals. In particular, dogs should never be offered any type of poultry bone. Chicken bones are soft and they can splinter. Although a bone splinter might get stuck in your dog's throat, the more common hazard is internal damage such as punctured intestines. Besides the damage bones can do internally, aggressive chewing on hard bones is a common cause of fractured teeth. Although veterinary dentists can now perform root canals for dogs, it is an expensive option for a preventable problem. If you must offer your dog bones, they should only be large beef knuckle bones, which do not readily splinter. Because natural bones are greasy, they are only suitable for chewing outside.

The Overweight Dog

Excessive weight puts a dog at increased risk for chronic health problems such as diabetes, heart disease, and arthritis. A plump Ridgeback is obvious because he does not have long fur to hide extra pounds. Once your dog is full grown, weighing him is the easiest way to keep track of his weight. In between weighing, you can still assess his weight. You should be able to feel your Ridgeback's ribs but not see them. When viewed from above, your Ridgeback should have an hourglass shape. He should have a slight indentation for his waist right behind his rib cage.

Preventing your dog from becoming overweight is easier than putting him on a reducing diet. Your dog can become anxious when it is necessary to feed him less, and it can be stressful to you when refusing his imploring looks for more food. Reduced-calorie foods are available for overweight dogs. These foods have fewer calories per serving than the manufacturer's regular brand. They tend to be lower in fat and higher in fiber than regular foods. An overweight dog also needs more exercise, not just a different food or less of his regular food.

Ridgebacks are not prone to excessive weight gain and do not tend to gain weight unless improperly fed. If you think your dog is overweight and you are feeding him properly or you have put him on a reducing diet but he still does not lose weight, then he should be examined by your veterinarian to determine whether there is a medical cause such as hypothyroidism.

MEDICAL PROBLEMS AND AILMENTS

Trust your instincts. If you think your Ridgeback is sick, she probably is. You should contact your veterinarian.

When to Visit the Veterinarian

Symptoms that indicate a visit to the veterinarian is necessary are lumps and bumps, behavior changes, an elevated temperature, long bouts of vomiting, diarrhea, or constipation. Loss of appetite is also a sign that something is amiss. Dogs do not get colds. If your dog has symptoms of a cold, such as runny eyes and nose, something is wrong and she should be seen by a veterinarian. Very often, waiting to treat a condition makes the recovery process longer and costlier. If a medication

A pack of Rhodesian Ridgebacks is a truly impressive sight, but caring for this many dogs requires great amounts of time and effort, not to mention the veterinary costs involved.

your veterinarian gives you does not work, you need to go back for further assistance.

Knowing how to take your dog's temperature can help you to determine whether she might be sick. Normal body temperature for dogs ranges from 100°F to 102.5°F (37.5°C to 39.2°C). A dog's temperature is taken rectally. Take her temperature while she is standing or lying down on her side, but do not let her sit on the thermometer.

A digital thermometer is often preferred because it beeps when the peak temperature is reached. Unlike a glass thermometer, there is little risk of accidentally breaking the thermometer. Use Vaseline to lubricate the tip of the thermometer. Lift your dog's tail, and gently insert the thermometer with a twisting motion about one-quarter of its length into the dog's rectum. Hold a glass thermometer in place for at least two minutes before reading it. Do not remove a digital thermometer until it beeps.

If your dog's temperature is higher then 103.5°F (39.7°C), she has a fever and should be examined by your veterinarian. If your dog's temperature is below normal and the thermometer is working, it can indicate poisoning and your veterinarian should be consulted. However, old dogs and some outdoor dogs often have temperatures below normal, especially when they first wake from a deep sleep. Be sure to rinse the thermometer in water followed by alcohol before returning it to its case.

Heatstroke

Dogs are not very efficient at cooling themselves. Although dogs perspire from their feet, they mainly cool themselves by panting. As a dog pants, body heat evaporates from her mouth. If the heat does not dissipate fast enough, the dog's body temperature can rise to a dangerous level.

Heatstroke is caused by exposure to high temperatures. Heatstroke can develop in only a few minutes and cause a dog's body temperature to soar. Signs of heatstroke include rapid noisy breathing, bright red gums, a red enlarged tongue, and thick or excessive saliva. The dog's eyes may be glazed and she will be listless. In some cases, the dog vomits and has diarrhea. As the condition progresses, the dog's pulse will be rapid and weak, followed by shock, coma, and death.

Heatstroke is a medical emergency. A dog with heatstroke can die if she is not quickly cooled. Depending on the circumstances, use towels soaked in cold water, a hose, or ice packs to lower your dog's body temperature immediately, but do not immerse her in ice water. If available, use a thermometer to monitor your dog's cooling body temperature. Once her temperature has dropped to 103°F (39°C), immediately take her to a veterinarian for further treatment.

Prevention of heatstroke is best. During hot weather, resist the urge to take your dog with you in the car, even for short errands. If you must travel in hot weather with your dog, be prepared with a cooler of ice water and some ice packs. Even so, you still must not leave her unattended in the car.

Heat exhaustion can occur while exercising on hot days. A dog with heat exhaustion may collapse, vomit, or have muscle cramps. Although they have short hair, Ridgebacks are still susceptible to heat exhaustion. A Ridgeback has a lot of heart and stamina and will keep exercising even when she is suffering. When it is too hot for you, it is definitely too hot for your Ridgeback. Remember that your dog cannot cool off as quickly as you can. Modify your exercise schedule to suit your dog's requirements. During hot weather, exercise you dog in the early morning or late evening. Be especially careful with older and overweight dogs, since they are particularly susceptible to heat exhaustion.

Frostbite

Ridgebacks have a short coat, and those in good condition lack a thick layer of insulating fat beneath the coat. Nonetheless, most individuals tolerate cold weather well and enjoy rolling in fresh snow. As long as they are moving, they can stay warm. But Ridgebacks can become miserable if made to stay outdoors or inactive in cold snowy weather. In very cold weather, Ridgebacks can develop frostbite on their ears, tail, toes, and genitals. Suspect frostbite if the area is very cold and pale white. Be aware in freezing temperatures not to expose your Ridgeback for too long at one time. Treat frostbitten areas with warm compresses. Do not rub frostbitten extremities, as doing so can damage the tissue. Frostbite can be painful. Follow-up treatment should be provided by your dog's veterinarian. On very cold days, a dog coat can provide your Ridgeback with extra warmth.

Vomiting and Diarrhea

At some point in her life, your dog will experience vomiting or diarrhea. Most bouts pass quickly and do not require veterinary treatment. Vomiting can occur for minor reasons, such as eating something disagreeable or eating too fast, but it can also be a result of infection, internal parasites, or digestive diseases. Persistent vomiting is serious, and your dog should be seen by her veterinarian.

Loose or watery bowel movements might be the result of your dog having eaten something disagreeable or a minor intestinal upset. However, diarrhea is also a symptom of infectious diseases and other ailments. If the diarrhea persists for 48 hours and is accompanied by other symptoms, such as lack of appetite, vomiting, or fever, it can indicate a serious illness that requires veterinary care. In particular, your dog should be examined by a veterinarian if she seems to be getting worse or if blood or mucus is in her droppings. A dog can become dehydrated and lethargic from diarrhea that lasts for several days.

TIP

Human Medications

Never give your dog any human medications without first checking with your veterinarian. Several common medicines for people, such as acetaminophen (Tylenol), are toxic to dogs. However, your veterinarian might recommend human over-the-counter medications for some ailments that affect your dog. Follow his or her instructions exactly.

For both vomiting and diarrhea, treatment typically entails withholding food for 12 to 24 hours. This fast is followed by several small bland meals of cooked white rice with cooked chicken or hamburger for one or two days. Then return your dog to her regular food.

External Parasites

Parasites are organisms that survive by living and feeding on other organisms. Fleas, ticks, and mites are external parasites that live on or within a dog's skin. These pests are detrimental to a dog's health. Parasites can spread disease and even transmit other types of parasites to a dog. If left untreated, parasites can be a serious problem.

Fleas are the most common parasites that affect dogs. Fleas make dogs miserable, and a dog's constant scratching can annoy his owner as well as make his owner feel guilty. Heavy flea infestations can cause anemia, and fleas are also vectors for tapeworms. Some dogs are highly allergic to fleas, which can cause a condition called flea allergy dermatitis. A flea injects saliva when it bites, which causes severe skin irritation and scratching. For dogs with an allergy to fleas, one flea bite can send them into a frenzy of chewing and scratching.

Fleas thrive in warm environments with high humidity. Thus, fleas are a severe, year-round problem in some parts of the country. In other regions, fleas are a problem only during the warmer part of the year. Because fleas do not typically occur above 5,000 feet (1.5 km) in elevation, dog owners in these areas do not have to contend with fleas.

Just because your dog scratches herself, it does not mean she has fleas. Fleas concentrate in areas that dogs cannot readily reach with their nails or teeth, such as above their tail and underneath their collar. If you are uncertain whether your dog has fleas, part the hair in these areas and look for the small, fast-moving fleas or search for crumbly black specks that are flea droppings. When moistened with water, these flecks will turn red because they contain the digested blood excreted by fleas. You can also roll your dog onto her back and look for fleas on her belly and groin. Keep in mind that scientists estimate that for every adult flea on a dog, there are 100 to 200 immature fleas in various other stages of the flea life cycle in the immediate environment.

The life cycle of the flea includes egg, larva, pupa, and adult. The adult flea drinks your dog's blood. After mating, the female flea lays her eggs on your dog or on her bedding. Flea eggs are found wherever your dog spends time. The transformation from egg to adult usually takes between two to four weeks. However, fleas are hardy. Under optimal conditions, the adults can survive for months without eating

Breaking the life cycle is an effective means to control fleas. Depending on where you live, flea control might be a year-round battle. If fleas are a seasonal problem, the most effective approach is to begin your flea control regimen at least one month before fleas become a problem.

Because the flea life cycle takes place both on and off your dog, you must treat both your dog and her environment, which includes your

If your Ridgeback spends a great deal of time outdoors, check him regularly for ticks and other external parasites.

Paying attention to your dog's demeanor can help you identify possible health problems.

home and backyard. If you live in an urban area and your neighbors also have dogs, try to coordinate yard treatment with them to reduce potential sources of reinfestation.

In the last decade, a new generation of sophisticated flea products was developed that made flea control more convenient, as well as safer and more effective. They are often called *spot on* because a single drop of the product is applied to the back of your dog's neck, typically only once a month. The product moves across the skin and wicks through the dog's coat to provide protection. Several brands are available only through your veterinarian, but other brands are sold at pet stores. Each brand typically relies on a different active ingredient and mode of action. Some kill the adults on contact, some kill fleas after they have ingested blood from the dog, and some prevent flea eggs and larvae from hatching

Consult with your veterinarian as to the best products and methods to use for your situation. Choosing the correct product is important. Some products are water soluble. If your Ridgeback regularly swims, you should use a product that will not come off when she gets wet. For dogs with flea allergy dermatitis, the best product to use is one that kills the fleas before they bite the dog. To be effective, you must be consistent and give the product(s) enough time to work.

Many pet owners prefer "natural" remedies for flea control. Unfortunately, herbal remedies

Rhodesian Ridgebacks enjoy snow, but their coats do not provide much insulation.

such as vitamin B, garlic, and brewer's yeast are not effective against fleas. However, vacuuming your house, especially where your dog spends her time, and washing your dog's bedding at least once a week are natural flea-control methods. For flea control outside your house,

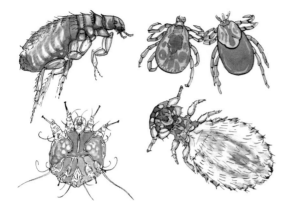

Fleas, ticks, mites, and lice are all external parasites that can infest dogs.

one company offers a natural product that consists of nematodes. These microscopic organisms prey on flea larvae in your yard, which helps to reduce the potential flea population.

Flea combing your Ridgeback for a few minutes every day is also a natural way to give your dog some immediate relief from biting fleas. The fleas get trapped in the fine teeth of the comb and can then be killed with your fingers or washed into a cup of water with bleach or detergent. Using a flea comb can help you monitor the success of your flea control program.

Ticks are a concern because they can transmit serious diseases to both dogs and people. Depending on their geographic range, ticks can carry the infectious organisms that cause Lyme disease, ehrlichiosis, and Rocky Mountain spotted fever. Ticks suck blood from their hosts for hours or even for several days and often become grotesquely enlarged from their blood meals. After feeding, most drop off the dog and molt; mature females then lay their eggs. The ticks then remain in your home or yard until they are ready for their next meal.

When taking your dog into areas with ticks, temporarily using a flea and tick collar can help reduce the number of ticks that climb onto your dog. Several of the flea-control spot-on products also kill ticks. However, some products do not work until after a tick has bitten your dog. Therefore, you should routinely examine your dog for ticks when returning from a hike in a tick-infested area. The Ridgeback's short coat makes finding ticks relatively easy. Be sure to check both behind and inside her ears. A flea comb is useful for finding ticks, but be careful not to rip out a tick imbedded in your dog. If the tick's mouthparts are left behind, they can cause an infection.

If you find a tick biting your dog, do not remove it with your bare hands. The spirochete that causes Lyme disease can enter through any opening you might have on your skin. Apply some alcohol to the tick. The tick will be dead in a few minutes. Use tweezers to grasp the tick as close to the skin as possible and pull steadily to remove it. You can examine large ticks after removal to assess whether you have removed the mouthparts as well.

A vaccination for Lyme disease is available. However, veterinarians typically recommend it only if there is a high incidence of Lyme disease in your area. If your dog becomes sick shortly after you removed a biting tick, consult your veterinarian. Treatment for tick-borne illnesses is most successful if diagnosis and treatment begins right away.

Mange mites: Canine scabies is also known as sarcoptic mange. It is caused by microscopic mites that burrow into the dog's skin, causing severe itchiness. These mites are not visible to

Internal parasites should be diagnosed and treated by your veterinarian.

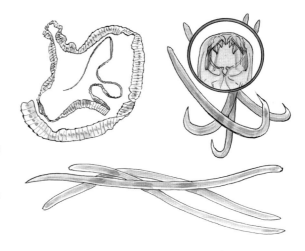

the naked eye. Sarcoptic mites prefer the skin of the ears, elbows, hocks, and face. Symptoms include hair loss, crusty skin, and red itchy bumps. Because of the intense itchiness, some dogs self-traumatize affected areas by vigorous scratching and biting. When untreated, the dog's skin thickens and feels leathery. The dog can also develop a strong odor. These mites can also affect people, especially after prolonged contact with an infested dog.

Demodectic mange is caused by a microscopic mite that is normally present in small numbers in the hair follicles of most healthy dogs. (The mites are not visible to the naked eye.) Demodectic mange is thought to be associated with a depression of the dog's immune system from causes such as poor nutrition, illness, or shipping. It is most common in dogs younger than two years of age. Typical signs are patches of hair loss, reddening of the skin, and scaling. This condition does not always cause itching or irritation. Areas commonly affected by demodectic mites include the eyes, corners of the mouth, and the front legs.

Mites are not seasonal and can affect your dog at any time of the year. For all types of mite infestations, veterinarian diagnosis and treatment is required. A veterinarian will identify the type of mite by examining skin scrapings under a microscope. Sometimes mites cannot be found in the scrapings, but based on the dog's symptoms, treatment to eliminate mites will be given anyway. When needed, a veterinarian can also prescribe an anti-inflammatory medication to relieve the dog's itchy condition.

Internal Parasites

Roundworms, hookworms, tapeworms, and heartworms are the most common internal parasites that affect dogs. If undetected and left untreated, internal parasites can be a serious problem. Because the eggs of many species of internal parasites are shed in a dog's droppings, it is important to pick up your dog's droppings to limit potential sources of infestation. Part of a new puppy checkup entails bringing a stool sample that is checked for the eggs of internal parasites. Your veterinarian will recommend whether annual checks are necessary. For all cases of internal parasites, rely on your veterinarian to diagnose and treat the condition with a deworming medication. Heartworm infection, which is transmitted from dog to dog by the bite of an infected mosquito, is preventable with the use of preventive medication. Your veterinarian will advise whether your dog should receive heartworm preventative.

Immunizations

Vaccines are given to prevent your dog from getting infectious diseases. Most vaccines are designed to prevent viral infections. Vaccinations are necessary because no drug is totally effective at curing viral infections once they are established.

For the first few weeks of your puppy's life, the antibodies present in the colostrum (first milk) from the mother will protect the puppy. However, if the mother has not developed immunity, neither will the puppy. For protection against numerous infectious diseases, puppies are typically immunized against distemper, hepatitis, parvovirus, parainfluenza, coronavirus, and leptospirosis. Referred to as the puppy series, the shots are usually administered over a period of two to four months. Your Ridgeback puppy's first inoculation might have already been administered by the breeder or it might need to be given by your veterinarian. Your vet will provide you with a schedule for

Puppies should only play with adult dogs that have received all their immunizations.

your puppy's vaccinations. After the series is complete, an adult dog receives an annual vaccine booster for these same diseases.

Viral vaccines are not always completely effective, and even dogs that have been vaccinated might still be susceptible to the virus. Factors such as nutritional status, age, and general health of the dog affect vaccine efficacy. Your veterinarian can discuss any mitigating factors with you. In many cases, some vaccines provide immunity for several years, but most dogs still receive annual boosters. Instead of yearly vaccinations, some dog owners have veterinarians perform annual blood tests (called titers) that measure the dog's level of immunity. Such tests are typically performed for dogs that previously experienced an adverse reaction to vaccination or are at genetic or physiological risk for reactions. If the level of immunity to infectious agents is too low, the dog is given the necessary vaccination.

Rabies: Between three to four months of age, your puppy is given his first rabies vaccine. A second rabies vaccine is given when the young dog is between 12 and 15 months of age. Different states have different requirements for revaccinations, from every year to every three years.

Bordetella is also called kennel cough. It is a highly contagious disease with symptoms that include coughing, sneezing, hacking, and retching. It can last for several days to several weeks. Kennel cough is rarely a simple infection. Other infectious pathogens, such as the parainfluenza virus, are often involved. A vaccine is available, but it does not protect against all strains of this condition because it is a complex infection. The vaccination should be given routinely to dogs that come in contact with other dogs (e.g., boarding kennels, shows, and dog parks).

Vaccinations are available for other ailments, including *Giardia,* a protozoan that affects the digestive system. Your veterinarian can advise whether other vaccinations are recommended for your Ridgeback.

Hereditary Ailments

Like all purebred dogs, the Ridgeback is subject to certain hereditary ailments and conditions.

Dermoid sinus is a potentially fatal condition that is present at birth in some Ridgeback puppies. A dermoid sinus is a hollow tube of skin that begins on the surface of the dog's skin and grows down to the dog's spinal cord. However, there is great variability, and some sinuses do not extend to the surface of the

Make it a habit to check your Ridgeback's ears for dirt, parasites, and discharge.

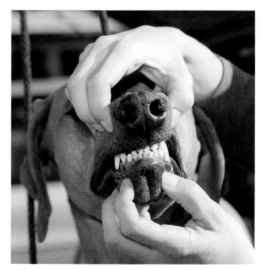

Cleaning your dog's teeth and checking for wear and fractures should be a normal part of your routine.

dog's skin. A dermoid sinus may become blocked with hair and skin debris, which leads to fluid collection in the sinus, infection of the spinal cord, and painful death. Dermoid sinus is most common along the spinal column on a puppy's neck, back, and tail, although it is also found in other locations such as the skull.

A dermoid sinus can be felt on a newborn puppy by palpating and shaving the suspected area. Puppies diagnosed with the condition are usually euthanized. Some dermoid sinuses can be surgically removed, but those that directly affect the spinal cord are almost impossible to remove. The operation is somewhat exploratory, because it is not possible to determine what type of dermoid sinus the puppy has until surgery. Even after surgery, the dermoid sinus can sometimes grow back. In addition, surgery is expensive, and caring for the surgical site can be difficult. Because the condition is inherited, dogs who have successfully had a dermoid sinus removed should be spayed or neutered.

As long as you purchase your puppy from a responsible breeder who screens his or her puppies for dermoid sinuses, you should not have

Pet Health Insurance

In cases of catastrophic illness or accident, pet health insurance can be a lifesaver for owners who might otherwise have to put down their dog because they could not afford his medical treatment. Pet insurance can be complicated, involving waiting periods, deductibles, pay-out limits, and exclusions. Ask your veterinarian for suggestions on a plan and research your options thoroughly.

to be concerned with this condition. However, many backyard breeders do not have the experience to detect this condition successfully, and you take a risk if you buy from them.

Bloat, also called gastric dilatation-volvulus (GDV), is a serious, life-threatening condition that can affect Ridgebacks and other deep-chested, large, and giant-breed dogs. The exact causes of this condition are not known. However, it usually occurs when a dog overeats, bolts food, swallows air, drinks large amounts of water immediately after eating, exercises vigorously before or after meals, and/or from stressful situations that cause the dog to become agitated. Air and fluid accumulate in the stomach that the dog cannot relieve by burping or vomiting. As gases build up, the stomach can rotate and block circulation.

Signs of bloat usually occur within a few hours after eating and include repeated attempts to vomit with only thick, stringy saliva being produced. Abdominal swelling occurs immediately behind the rib cage. The dog suffers severe pain and is restless at first but will soon begin to stagger and then become lethargic. The pain exacerbates as the stomach continues to inflate with gas and fluid. In severe cases, the bloated stomach might pouch out on one side of the dog's abdomen. The condition rapidly progresses. An affected dog will exhibit signs of shock, such as pale gums, weakness, and increased heart and respiration rate, and will eventually become comatose. Any of these symptoms constitute an extreme emergency, and you should immediately take your dog to a veterinary hospital for emergency treatment.

Unless immediately treated by a veterinarian, the dog will die. If time allows, a veterinarian will take X rays to determine whether the stomach has rotated. Treatment consists of passing a tube into the stomach to remove the air and fluid, or if the stomach has rotated, surgery is necessary to save the dog's life. If surgery relieves the stomach torsion and circulation to the stomach and small intestine is reestablished, most veterinarians will surgically anchor the dog's stomach in place to help prevent the disease from recurring. Even when the treatment is successful, death can occur up to a week later because of shock or complications.

Bloat is expensive to treat and can be fatal even with veterinary treatment; prevention is best. Instead of one large meal, feed at least two meals a day, one in the morning and one in the evening, or even better, feed several small meals throughout the day. Soak your dog's dry kibble with water to prevent her from bolting her food. Limit your dog's access to water immediately after eating. Do not exercise your dog for two hours before and after she eats. Check the American Kennel Club's (AKC) web site *www.akc.org* for information on bloat as more is learned about the causes and prevention of this ailment.

Hip dysplasia is a hereditary disease that can affect Ridgebacks. In affected dogs, the ball and socket joints of one or both hips develop abnormally, which allows the ball end of the thighbone to separate from the hip joint. This causes degeneration and erosion of the joint cartilage and bony surfaces. This condition can be painful, cause lameness, and reduce activity levels. Rapid growth, overfeeding, and excessive exercise can influence the severity of the disease.

Hip dysplasia can suddenly appear in a young dog, or it may gradually appear as the dog matures. The condition is diagnosed by X rays of the hip joints. The disease progresses slowly, and no cure is available. Treatment of hip dysplasia can involve moderate daily exercise to help strengthen the muscles and tendons underlying and supporting the affected joint, anti-inflammatory medications to help relieve pain, surgery to clean and rebuild the joints to help reduce pain and improve function, or total hip replacement. However, surgery should be carefully considered, as it is painful and expensive.

The Orthopedic Foundation for Animals (OFA) has established guidelines for testing and detecting hip dysplasia in dogs two years old or older. The OFA reviews X rays of a dog's hips. If the X rays show no evidence of the condition, the OFA will certify that the dog is free of the condition. It is highly recommended that all dogs used for breeding have their hips x-rayed and rated by the OFA at age two before being bred.

Elbow dysplasia is a hereditary, degenerative joint disease of the elbow. It is a problem of young dogs during skeletal development and affects a small percentage of Ridgebacks. The ailment causes lameness and osteoarthritis if not treated. In some cases, flaps of cartilage or fragments of bones irritate and abrade the elbow joint. Various types of surgery may be performed to relieve the condition. Despite surgery, some lameness often persists. As with hip dysplasia, the OFA can review and evaluate X rays of a dog's elbows. Certification of elbow conformation is based on pass or fail. Buying a Ridgeback from a responsible breeder who screens his or her dogs minimizes the chances of your dog being affected with elbow dysplasia.

Hypothyroidism is a hormonal disease caused by a deficiency of thyroid hormone,

Senior Ridgebacks will slow down and be content with less vigorous exercise.

A healthy Ridgeback is energetic and alert.

which is itself composed of two major hormones. Decreased thyroid function usually occurs when the thyroid gland is destroyed. Causes of damage include immune-mediated inflammation of the thyroid gland or cancer, or the condition may be congenital (existing since birth). Symptoms include a reluctance to exercise, mental lethargy, weight gain (without an increase in appetite or food intake), and a dull, dry coat. Other signs include dark pigmentation of the skin, hair loss, and scaly skin. These symptoms are often gradual in appearance. An affected Ridgeback usually does not show symptoms until she is between four to ten years old. A blood test that assesses the level of thyroid hormone, along with the above symptoms, is used to diagnose hypothyroidism. A Ridgeback with hypothyroidism is treated with synthetic thyroid pills, usually given twice a day. The medication must be continued throughout the dog's life. Once treatment has begun, the improvement in the dog's appearance and attitude is remarkable.

Eye Problems

Eye diseases are not generally a problem in Ridgebacks. However, two eye conditions that occur in Ridgebacks are cataracts and entropion.

A cataract causes all or part of the eye's clear lens to become opaque or cloudy. The cataract can appear as white flecks, or the entire eye can have a gray or blue cast. Depending on the size and location, a cataract can cause partial or complete loss of sight. Corrective surgery is usually recommended when the cataract causes blindness. Operations to remove cataracts can restore vision to nearly normal.

Cataracts that occur at an early age are usually inherited. The chances of your dog developing cataracts is reduced if you buy from a breeder whose dogs' eyes have been examined and cleared by a veterinary ophthalmologist affiliated with the Canine Eye Registration Foundation (CERF).

Entropion is a congenital condition in which the lower and/or upper eyelid rolls inward. The lashes and eyelid hairs rub the cornea, creating irritation and injury. Entropion can be corrected with surgery.

The Senior Dog

A Ridgeback's life expectancy is about 12 years. Generally, large dogs such as the Ridgebacks are considered senior dogs when they are seven years of age. A graying muzzle is the first obvious sign that your dog is getting older. Other changes are less obvious. Your Ridgeback should have annual or biannual visits to the veterinarian. These wellness checks can help to detect some ailments in their early stages, such as the cataracts that cause cloudy eyes in older dogs. Conditions detected in their early stages can be treated more successfully than those found when they are in advanced stages. Your veterinarian might recommend an annual blood profile and urinalysis to detect disorders of the kidneys and liver so that proper treatment can be initiated.

Older dogs sleep longer and more deeply. A Ridgeback used to sleeping on your bed might have more difficulty jumping on and off the bed. Place a thick foam, orthopedic bed designed to relieve the stress of arthritis and stiff joints next to your bed. This will give your senior dog a comfortable place to sleep while still feeling like part of the family. Many times the behavior changes that occur in old dogs are thought to be a natural consequence of old age. However, the dog might also be suffering from a painful medical condition that cannot be readily detected by you.

Older dogs slow down and are less active. However, they must still receive regular exercise, such as leisurely walks around the block or romps through fields. A consistent, moderate exercise regimen will help keep your dog's muscles toned, her joints flexible, and her bones strong. Young Ridgebacks can readily tolerate the weekend warrior lifestyle, whereby the weekday long walks around the block are replaced with arduous long-distance hikes on the weekend. Older dogs are less tolerant of inconsistent exercise regimes. Your senior might appear to have the heart to get up and go, but she does not have a young dog's endurance and is likely to return home stiff and in pain. While it can be difficult to leave your canine companion behind, it is the preferred option. Taking your senior for a shorter hike or walk before you go can ease your guilt and provide your dog with sufficient stimulus to keep her happy.

Because senior dogs are less active, their caloric intake must be correspondingly reduced to prevent weight gain. Obesity increases the risk of heart disease and puts more stress on the older dog's joints. An older dog who loses her appetite might need her teeth cleaned. Swollen gums and loose teeth can make eating painful. Anesthesia, which is required for professional cleaning, is riskier for older dogs, so be diligent about brushing your dog's teeth.

Grooming tasks, such as brushing and nail trimming, should not be neglected. Because she is less active, nail trimming might need to be done more frequently. Older dogs sometimes smell "doggy" as they age. This can be due to a skin condition called seborrhea. Brushing and occasional baths will reduce the smell, as will regularly washing her bedding. Problems with teeth, ears, urinary tract, and anal glands can also make an older dog smell. Unpleasant odors indicate a potential problem, and your veterinarian should be consulted.

Hearing and sight: With increasing age, a dog's sense of hearing and sight decline, as well as mental alertness. Senior Ridgebacks become less emotionally flexible and easily traumatized if left in unfamiliar surroundings such as a veterinary hospital or kennel. Some older dogs exhibit declining mental abilities that are similar to those seen in people with Alzheimer's. Called cognitive dysfunction syndrome (CDS), the changes are so similar that dogs are used as a model for understanding brain aging in humans and in developing treatments. Odd behaviors, such as barking at nothing or standing in the wrong place to go outside, can indicate CDS. A diet high in the right concentration of antioxidants has been found to prevent the changes in a dog's brain that cause CDS. Senile dogs fed these scientifically formulated foods become more lively, attentive, and responsive. Specialty diets rich in antioxidants are available by prescription from veterinarians for dogs with this condition. Besides diet, medications are available that help treat CDS.

A puppy often revives an older dog's interest in life, but the decision to get a new "replacement" dog while your present dog is growing older requires a thoughtful assessment of your senior dog's personality and condition. Not all dogs welcome a puppy, particularly "people dogs" who were never dog friendly to begin

with. Some medical conditions, such as arthritis, are painful, and make it less likely your dog will enjoy playing with a puppy. In such cases, provide your senior dog with a safe retreat from the boisterous attention of the puppy and do not allow the puppy to make your senior miserable with her rambunctious behavior.

Saying Good-bye

Most people hope their old dog passes away peacefully in his sleep. Some dogs do die this way, but most pet owners are faced with the painful decision of whether or not to put their dog to sleep. It is a major decision that can be very difficult to make. Good medical care can prolong the life of a treasured dog, but it can also extend it to the point where your dog's best interests are no longer served. Your veterinarian can help you assess the quality of your dog's life, especially if your dog is being treated for a fatal disease, such as an inoperable tumor.

The decision is easier to make when a dog has no chance of recovery and is in pain, but more ambiguous situations abound. Your instincts will help you to know when your dog is not happy and her pain overrides her ability to enjoy life. You will be able to endure your grief more easily when you and your family make the decision with love and care. Ask if your veterinarian is willing to come to your home for the procedure. The comfortable, familiar surroundings will make it easier for both you and your dog. Many people get a puppy a few years before this point is reached. The younger dog can help in the healing process and relieve the pain of an empty house.

Kennel Clubs

(Breed club officers normally change on a regular basis. For the most current information regarding breed club personnel, contact the national kennel club for the country you are interested in.)

American Kennel Club
5580 Centerview Drive
Suite 200
Raleigh, NC 27606
Phone: (919) 233-9767
Fax: (919) 233-3740
E-mail: info@akc.org
Web site: *www.akc.org*

Canadian Kennel Club
111 Eglington Avenue
Toronto 12, Ontario
Canada

The Kennel Club (England)
1-4 Clarges Street
Picadilly
London W7Y 8AB
England

Australian National Kennel Council
Royal Show Grounds
Ascot Vale
Victoria,
Australia

New Zealand Kennel Club
P.O. Box 523
Wellington 1
New Zealand

Rhodesian Ridgeback Club United States
P.O. Box 37
Columbia, MD 21045-0037

Rhodesian Ridgeback Rescue, Inc.
P.O. Box 5587
Washington, D.C. 20016-1187

For addresses of current club officers and local clubs, go online to: *rrcus.org.*

Lure Coursing

American Sighthound Field Association.org
www.akc.org

Lost Pet Registries

National Dog Registry
P.O. Box 118
Woodstock, NY 12498-0226
(800) 637-3647

Tattoo-A-Pet
1625 Emmons Avenue
Brooklyn, NY 11235
(800) TATTOOS

Home Again Microchip Registry (NDR)
(800) LONELY-ONE

Petfinders
368 High Street
Athol, NY 12810
(800) 223-4747

National Animal Poison Control Center
(900) 680-0000
($20.00 for five minutes and $2.95 per minute thereafter)

The Rhodesian Ridgeback is a good breed choice for someone who enjoys having a canine companion integrated into their active lifestyle.

Periodicals

Dog Fancy Magazine
P.O. Box 6050
Mission Viejo, CA 92690

Dog World
P.O. Box 6050
Mission Viejo, CA 92690

Books

Alderton, David. *The Dog Care Manual.* Hauppauge, New York: Barron's Educational Series, Inc., 1989.

American Kennel Club. *The Complete Dog Book,* 19th Edition Revised. New York: Howell Book House, 1997.

Baer Ted. *Communicating with Your Dog.* Hauppauge, New York: Barron's Educational Series, Inc., 1989.

Bailey, Gwen. *The Well-Behaved Dog.* Hauppauge, New York: Barron's Educational Series, Inc., 1998.

Coile, D. Caroline. *Show Me! A Dog Show Primer.* Hauppauge, New York: Barron's Educational Series, Inc., 1997.

Klever, Ulrich. *The Complete Book of Dog Care.* Hauppauge, New York: Barron's Educational Series, Inc., 1989.

Rice, Dan. *The Dog Handbook.* Hauppauge, New York: Barron's Educational Series, Inc., 1999.

Smith, Cheryl S., and Stephanie J. Tauton. *The Trick Is in the Training.* Hauppauge, New York: Barron's Educational Series, Inc., 1998.

Streitferdt, Uwe. *Healthy Dog, Happy Dog.* Hauppauge, New York: Barron's Educational Series, Inc., 1994.

Books on Rhodesian Ridgebacks

Bailey, Eileen. *The Rhodesian Ridgeback.* New York: Howell Book House, 2000.

Nicholson, Peter, and Parker, Janet. *The Complete Rhodesian Ridgeback,* 2nd Edition. Lydney, Gloucestershire, U.K.: Ringpress, 2001.

Carlson, Stig. *The Rhodesian Ridgeback Today.* New York: Howell Book House, 1999.

About the Author

Sue Fox is a wildlife biologist and a freelance writer. She has written numerous books about the care of a variety of pets and is a columnist for a pet trade magazine.

Photo Credits

Isabelle Francais, pages 12, 20 top left, 28, 33 bottom, 48, 53 top and bottom, 56, 60, 64 bottom left, 73 top and bottom, 76; Kent and Donna Dannen: pages 8 top and bottom left, 9 top left, top right and bottom, 20 bottom left, 21 top and bottom, 24 top and bottom, 25 top, 29, 32, 44 top and bottom left, 45 top, 49, 52 top left and right, bottom left, 61, 64 bottom right, 65 bottom right, 68, 72 top right, 80, 81 top and bottom, 84, 85 top and bottom, 88, 89, 93; Pets by Paulette: pages 3, 4, 5, 8 bottom right, 13 top left and right, bottom left and right, 16, 17, 20 right, 25 bottom, 33 top, 36, 37, 40, 41 top and bottom, 44 bottom right, 45 bottom left and right, 52 bottom right, 57, 64 top, 65 top and bottom left, 69, 72 top left and bottom, 77.

Acknowledgments

The author's sincere thanks go to the following people for their help: Mr. and Mrs. Joe Berger, Janice Horvat, Mike Isle, Bill Lewis, Carol Vesely, Debbie Wahley, as well as to all the other Rhodesian Ridgeback people who so generously shared their time and knowledge of the breed. The author would also like to thank Seymour Weiss, editor at Barron's, whose patience and considerable expertise contributed significantly to the quality of the manuscript.

Cover Photos

Pets by Paulette

All inquiries should be addressed to:
Barron's Educational Series, Inc.
250 Wireless Boulevard
Hauppauge, NY 11788
http://www.barronseduc.com

International Standard Book No. 0-7641-2376-9

Library of Congress Catalog Card No. 2003044407

Library of Congress Cataloging-in-Publication Data
Fox, Sue, 1962–
    Rhodesian ridgebacks : everything about
purchase, care, nutrition, behavior, and training /
Sue Fox ; illustrations by Michele Earle-Bridges.
        p. cm. — (A Complete pet owner's manual)
    Includes index.
    ISBN 0-7641-2376-9
    1. Rhodesian ridgeback. I. Title. II. Series.

SF429.R5F69 2003
636.753'6—dc21   2003044407

Printed in Hong Kong
9 8 7 6 5 4 3 2 1